Learning Data Structures: Efficient Programming with C++

A Step-by-Step Guide to Implementing Data Structures and Algorithms

BOOZMAN RICHARD

BOOKER BLUNT

Table of Content

TABLE OF CONTENTS

INTRODUCTION

DATA STRUCTURES EFFICIENT PROGRAMMING WITH C++

The web development landscape has evolved dramatically over the past decade, with JavaScript frameworks playing a pivotal role in shaping how developers build interactive, dynamic, and scalable applications. In this rapidly changing ecosystem, staying up to date with the latest frameworks and technologies is crucial to building high-performance web applications that meet user expectations for speed, reliability, and seamless experiences across devices.

This book, *Data structure Effcient Programming with c++*, is designed to be your comprehensive guide to mastering the most popular JavaScript frameworks used in modern web development. Whether you are just starting your journey into web development or you're a seasoned developer looking to deepen your knowledge, this book covers everything you need to know about **React**, **Angular**, and **Vue.js**. Each chapter is crafted to provide you with a clear understanding of the core concepts, best practices, and real-world examples, helping you build scalable, maintainable, and performant applications.

6

Why This Book Is Essential

The demand for rich, interactive web applications has never been higher. With the rise of Single Page Applications (SPAs), Progressive Web Apps (PWAs), and mobile-first design, developers must not only understand the principles of front-end development but also leverage modern JavaScript frameworks to enhance the user experience and meet the growing demands of today's digital world.

In this book, you will:

- Gain a deep understanding of **React**, **Angular**, and **Vue.js**, each of which has its unique strengths and weaknesses.
- Learn how to implement best practices for building fast, efficient, and secure web applications.
- Dive into advanced topics such as **state management**, **routing**, **service workers**, and **performance optimization**.
- Explore real-world examples of building web apps from scratch, including integrating APIs, securing user data, and optimizing performance.

- Get hands-on experience with building **Progressive Data structure Effcient Programming with c++ (SPAs)**, and mobile-first web solutions.

Whether you're looking to improve your skills in building scalable front-end applications or need to stay updated with the latest trends and technologies in web development, this book will serve as your essential companion.

What You Will Learn

In the first part of the book, we'll explore the foundational concepts of JavaScript frameworks. You'll get acquainted with the core principles behind **React**, **Angular**, and **Vue.js**, including their strengths, weaknesses, and appropriate use cases. We'll dive into the fundamentals of each framework, helping you choose the right tool for your next project.

Next, we will cover how to build real-world applications with these frameworks. You'll learn how to develop powerful web apps by creating dynamic user interfaces, managing state effectively, and implementing modern features like **routing**, **authentication**, and **data binding**. You'll also get hands-on experience building **single-page**

applications (SPAs) and integrating APIs to enhance the functionality of your app.

As we move deeper into advanced topics, the book will guide you through **state management** using libraries like **Redux** for React, **NgRx** for Angular, and **Vuex** for Vue.js. We'll also focus on performance optimization techniques such as **code splitting**, **lazy loading**, **caching**, and **progressive web apps (PWAs)** to ensure that your web apps perform at their best across all devices and network conditions.

Security is also a major concern when developing web applications. In this book, we'll explore how to protect your app from common vulnerabilities like **Cross-Site Scripting (XSS)**, **Cross-Site Request Forgery (CSRF)**, and **SQL Injection**. You'll learn how to implement secure authentication systems using **JWT** (JSON Web Tokens) and other modern techniques to safeguard your app's data and user privacy.

The final section of the book covers best practices and strategies for maintaining and evolving your web apps. We'll focus on **test-driven development (TDD)**, **unit testing**, and **end-to-end testing** with tools like **Jest, Karma,** and **Protractor**. We'll also discuss how to stay up to date with the latest trends and frameworks in the JavaScript ecosystem, ensuring your skills remain relevant in the ever-changing world of web development.

Who This Book Is For

This book is intended for developers of all experience levels who want to master modern JavaScript frameworks. Whether you are:

- A **beginner** looking to get started with React, Angular, or Vue.js, and want to learn the fundamentals of web development with modern frameworks.
- An **intermediate developer** who wants to deepen your understanding of state management, routing, testing, and performance optimization.
- An **experienced developer** seeking to stay updated on the latest tools, best practices, and trends in JavaScript frameworks, and how to build scalable, secure, and high-performance web applications.

Why React, Angular, and Vue.js?

The three frameworks covered in this book—**React**, **Angular**, and **Vue.js**—are the most widely used and popular choices for building web applications today. Each framework has unique features, and understanding their strengths and use cases will help you choose the right one for your project.

- **React**: Known for its simplicity and flexibility, React is a **JavaScript library** for building user interfaces. Its component-based architecture and virtual DOM make it highly efficient for rendering dynamic UIs, and it is widely adopted for creating modern, fast web applications.
- **Angular**: Angular is a **full-fledged framework** that provides everything you need for building large-scale web applications. With built-in tools like **dependency injection**, **routing**, and **forms management**, Angular is perfect for building complex, enterprise-level apps.
- **Vue.js**: Vue is a **progressive framework** that is both easy to learn and flexible enough to scale for large applications. It combines the best features of both React and Angular, offering an approachable

11

learning curve with powerful tools for building dynamic, modern web apps.

By the end of this book, you'll have a solid understanding of these frameworks and the ability to build robust, production-ready web apps with them.

Conclusion

The world of JavaScript frameworks is constantly evolving, and staying up-to-date with the latest tools and techniques is essential for becoming a proficient web developer. *Data structure Effcient Programming with c++* offers a detailed, hands-on guide to building modern web applications that are fast, scalable, and secure. By mastering these frameworks, you'll be equipped to tackle any web development challenge and stay at the forefront of the ever-changing landscape of web technologies.

Whether you're building a personal project or working on an enterprise-level application, the skills and knowledge you gain from this book will serve as a solid foundation for your future web development career. Let's dive in and explore the power of **React**, **Angular**, and **Vue.js**, and start building modern web apps that users love!

CHAPTER 1

INTRODUCTION TO DATA STRUCTURES AND ALGORITHMS

Overview of Data Structures and Their Importance in Programming

Data structures are fundamental concepts in computer science that allow us to organize, store, and manage data efficiently. The choice of data structure impacts how easily and quickly we can access, modify, and store data.

At a high level, data structures can be categorized into two types:

1. **Primitive Data Structures**: These are basic data types provided by programming languages, such as integers, floats, characters, and booleans.
2. **Non-Primitive Data Structures**: These are more complex structures that allow us to organize data in ways that suit specific needs. Examples include arrays, linked lists, stacks, queues, and trees.

Why are data structures important? In programming, they are the backbone of every application. They help in:

- **Efficient Data Storage**: Organizing data in a way that allows for fast retrieval and modification.
- **Improved Performance**: Choosing the right data structure optimizes memory usage and processing speed.
- **Solving Complex Problems**: Many algorithms require data to be stored in specific ways to function correctly and efficiently.

Without data structures, even the most powerful algorithms would be inefficient and impractical for real-world use cases.

Explanation of the Relationship Between Data Structures and Algorithms

While data structures are used to organize data, **algorithms** are sets of instructions designed to manipulate that data to solve specific problems. The two are intrinsically linked:

- **Data Structures** define how data is stored, accessed, and modified.
- **Algorithms** define the process of solving problems using data.

A simple analogy is comparing data structures to a **container** and algorithms to a **tool** used to manipulate the contents of that container. The more appropriate the data structure, the easier it is to implement algorithms that operate on that structure efficiently.

14

For example:

- **Sorting algorithms** (like quicksort or merge sort) depend heavily on how data is organized.
- **Searching algorithms** (like binary search) can only be efficient if the data is stored in a sorted structure, such as an array or tree.

Real-World Use Cases Where Data Structures Solve Complex Problems

In real-world applications, data structures are essential for handling and solving complex problems. Here are a few examples:

1. **Social Media Feeds**:
   - **Problem**: Showing users the most relevant posts in real time based on their preferences.
   - **Solution**: Social media platforms use **priority queues** and **hash tables** to organize and quickly access posts by relevance, likes, and time.
   - **Data Structure**: A hash table can be used for quick lookup of user preferences, while a priority queue might help rank posts based on factors like user engagement.
2. **Navigation Systems (GPS)**:

- o **Problem**: Finding the shortest path from one location to another in a complex network of roads.

- o **Solution**: Navigation apps use **graphs** (specifically directed and weighted graphs) where intersections are nodes and roads are edges, and **Dijkstra's algorithm** or *A search algorithm** is used to calculate the shortest path.

- o **Data Structure**: A graph stores all locations and connections, and algorithms like Dijkstra's help find the optimal route.

3. **E-Commerce Platforms**:

- o **Problem**: Recommending products based on user behavior and preferences.

- o **Solution**: E-commerce platforms use **trees** and **graphs** to represent hierarchical product categories and to track customer preferences, helping to suggest items effectively.

- o **Data Structure**: A decision tree might help in predicting customer choices, while a graph can represent product relationships and recommendations.

4. **Search Engines**:

- o **Problem**: Returning relevant search results to users in real-time.

o **Solution**: Search engines use **inverted indices**, which are a form of hash table, to quickly retrieve documents containing the queried terms.

o **Data Structure**: The inverted index stores words and the list of documents they appear in, allowing for fast text search and ranking.

These real-world examples highlight how the right choice of data structure can vastly improve the efficiency of solving everyday problems.

Basic Introduction to C++ and How It Is Used for Implementing Data Structures

C++ is one of the most widely used programming languages when it comes to implementing data structures due to its efficiency and fine-grained control over system resources. It combines the power of **procedural** and **object-oriented** programming, making it well-suited for developing complex data structure operations.

In C++, data structures are typically implemented using:

- **Arrays**: For storing a fixed number of elements.
- **Classes** and **Structures**: For defining custom data types such as linked lists, stacks, and queues.
- **Pointers and Dynamic Memory Allocation**: For implementing more complex data structures like linked

lists, trees, and graphs that require dynamic memory allocation.

C++ Standard Library (STL) also provides ready-made implementations of some of the most common data structures like:

- **Vectors** (dynamic arrays),
- **Lists** (doubly linked lists),
- **Stacks**, **Queues**, and **Priority Queues**,
- **Maps** (key-value pairs, similar to hash tables).

The real power of C++ lies in its ability to manipulate data structures at a low level, with direct control over memory and system resources. This makes it ideal for both beginner learning and advanced data structure applications in performance-critical software.

Conclusion

This chapter serves as a foundational introduction to data structures, setting the stage for a deeper dive into their implementation in C++. You have learned the importance of data structures, how they relate to algorithms, and their real-world applications. In the coming chapters, we'll explore various data structures and their implementations, with a strong focus on practical, real-world examples that showcase how they can optimize performance and solve complex problems efficiently.

Let's begin your journey into the world of data structures and algorithms with C++.

CHAPTER 2

SETTING UP YOUR DEVELOPMENT ENVIRONMENT

In this chapter, we will walk through the steps necessary to set up your development environment for C++ programming. This includes installing a C++ compiler and Integrated Development Environment (IDE), writing your first C++ program, setting up version control with GitHub, and exploring basic debugging techniques. These are foundational skills you'll need as you embark on learning and implementing data structures and algorithms in C++.

Installing C++ Compilers and IDEs (e.g., Code::Blocks, Visual Studio)

To begin programming in C++, you need both a **compiler** and an **IDE**. The compiler translates your code into machine language that the computer can execute, and the IDE provides you with the tools to write, compile, and debug your code more efficiently.

Step 1: Choosing a C++ Compiler

- The C++ compiler you use depends on your operating system. Some common compilers include:

20

- o **GCC (GNU Compiler Collection)** for Linux and MacOS.
- o **MinGW** for Windows.
- o **Clang** for macOS (a part of the Xcode Command Line Tools).

Most IDEs, like **Code::Blocks** or **Visual Studio**, include a built-in compiler, so you don't have to install one separately.

Step 2: Installing Code::Blocks Code::Blocks is an open-source IDE that is simple to use and is suitable for beginners.

1. **Download** Code::Blocks from Code::Blocks website.
2. **Install** the IDE: Choose the version that includes the **MinGW** compiler (for Windows users). This will automatically install the necessary compiler along with the IDE.
3. Once installed, **launch Code::Blocks**, and you're ready to start coding in C++.

Step 3: Installing Visual Studio (Alternative) Visual Studio is a more feature-rich IDE and is widely used in professional environments.

1. Download Visual Studio from the official website.
2. During installation, make sure to select the **Desktop development with C++** workload. This will include the

Visual C++ compiler, which is required for compiling C++ programs.

3. After installation, launch Visual Studio and create a new C++ project to begin coding.

Writing and Compiling Your First C++ Program

Now that you've set up your development environment, let's write and compile your first C++ program.

Step 1: Writing the Program

1. **Open your IDE** (Code::Blocks or Visual Studio).
2. Create a new project:
   - In **Code::Blocks**, go to **File > New > Project**, and select a console application in C++.
   - In **Visual Studio**, go to **File > New > Project**, select **Console App**, and choose C++.
3. Replace the default code in the main file with the following simple "Hello, World!" program:

cpp

```
#include <iostream>

int main() {
    // Output a message to the console
```

```
    std::cout    <<    "Hello,    World!"    <<
std::endl;
    return 0;
}
```

Step 2: Compiling the Program

1. **Compile and run the program**:
   o In **Code::Blocks**, press **F9** or click on the green "Build and Run" button.
   o In **Visual Studio**, press **Ctrl+F5** to run without debugging or **F5** to run with debugging.

The program should output `Hello, World!` to the console. This basic program serves as an introduction to the C++ syntax and compiling process.

Setting Up Version Control with GitHub

Version control allows you to keep track of changes made to your code over time and collaborate with others. **Git** is the most widely used version control system, and **GitHub** is a platform that hosts your code repositories and facilitates collaboration.

Step 1: Installing Git

- If you haven't installed Git yet, visit Git's official website to download and install it.

23

- After installation, you can verify it by typing `git --version` in your terminal or command prompt to check that Git was successfully installed.

Step 2: Setting Up GitHub

1. Create a **GitHub** account at github.com.
2. After signing in, create a new repository by clicking on the **New** button on the GitHub homepage.
3. Follow these steps to connect your local code to GitHub:
    - Initialize a Git repository in your project folder by running:

    bash

    ```
    git init
    ```

    - Add your files to the staging area:

    bash

    ```
    git add .
    ```

    - Commit the changes:

    bash

    ```
    git commit -m "Initial commit"
    ```

o   Connect your local repository to GitHub:

```bash

git       remote       add       origin
https://github.com/yourusername/you
r-repository.git
```

o   Push your code to GitHub:

```bash

git push -u origin master
```

Now, your project is safely stored on GitHub, and you can easily track and collaborate on your code. Every time you make changes, use `git add`, `git commit`, and `git push` to save your progress.

Simple Debugging Techniques

Debugging is an essential skill in programming. It helps you identify and fix errors in your code. Here are a few basic techniques to get started with debugging in C++:

Step 1: Using Print Statements The simplest form of debugging is inserting print statements (e.g., `std::cout`) into your program to display variable values at various points. This helps you understand what's going on and where things might be going wrong.

25

For example, if you're trying to find an error in a loop, print out the value of a variable inside the loop:

cpp

```cpp
for (int i = 0; i < 5; i++) {
    std::cout << "i = " << i << std::endl;
}
```

Step 2: Using the Debugger Both **Code::Blocks** and **Visual Studio** have built-in debuggers that allow you to set breakpoints, step through your code, and inspect the values of variables at each step.

- **Setting Breakpoints**: In your IDE, click on the margin next to the line number to set a breakpoint. When the program reaches that point, it will pause, allowing you to check the values of variables.
- **Stepping Through Code**: Once the program pauses at a breakpoint, you can step through each line of code using **Step Over** (F10) and **Step Into** (F11) commands.
- **Inspecting Variables**: Most IDEs allow you to hover over variables or use a **Watch Window** to view their values during debugging.

Step 3: Common Debugging Practices

- **Check for common errors**: Typo in variable names, incorrect operators, or wrong function arguments.
- **Test with different inputs**: Try edge cases or boundary conditions to see how the program behaves with extreme values.
- **Use assertions**: Use `assert` statements in your code to verify that assumptions about the program's state hold true.

Conclusion

By the end of this chapter, you should have a working C++ development environment, have written and compiled your first C++ program, be able to use GitHub for version control, and know basic debugging techniques. These are foundational skills that will help you as you dive into more complex topics like data structures and algorithms. With your setup complete, you're ready to tackle the challenges of learning efficient programming with C++.

CHAPTER 3

UNDERSTANDING BIG O NOTATION

In this chapter, we'll dive into **Big O notation**, an essential concept for understanding the efficiency of algorithms. By the end of this chapter, you'll know how to analyze the time and space complexity of algorithms, compare different algorithms, and understand the importance of optimization, especially in real-world applications.

Introduction to Time and Space Complexity

When you write an algorithm, two of the most important things to consider are **time complexity** and **space complexity**. These describe how the algorithm's resource usage (time and memory) grows as the size of the input increases.

1. **Time Complexity**: This measures the amount of time an algorithm takes to complete as a function of the size of the input. It gives you an idea of how the running time increases as the input size grows.

   o **Example**: If an algorithm takes 1 millisecond to process 100 items, but 10 milliseconds to process

28

1,000 items, we are looking at an algorithm where time grows with the input size.

2. **Space Complexity**: This measures the amount of memory an algorithm uses as a function of the size of the input. It helps you understand how much additional memory your program will require while executing.

   ○ **Example**: If an algorithm stores a of all the elements in an array, its space complexity will increase as the size of the array increases.

Both time and space complexity are critical for evaluating the efficiency of algorithms. A more efficient algorithm will minimize both time and space usage, especially as the input size increases.

Analyzing Algorithms Using Big O Notation

Big O notation provides a way to describe the upper bound of an algorithm's time and space complexity. It allows you to express the worst-case scenario for how an algorithm's performance will scale with larger inputs. Big O notation focuses on how the runtime (or memory usage) grows relative to the input size, ignoring constant factors.

Here are the most common Big O complexities:

1. **O(1)** – Constant time: The algorithm's runtime does not depend on the input size. It takes the same amount of time to execute, regardless of the input size.

   o **Example**: Accessing an element in an array by index.

2. **O(log n)** – Logarithmic time: The algorithm's runtime grows logarithmically with the input size. As the input size doubles, the time increases by a constant amount.

   o **Example**: Binary search in a sorted array.

3. **O(n)** – Linear time: The algorithm's runtime grows linearly with the input size. If you double the size of the input, the time doubles as well.

   o **Example**: Linear search in an unsorted array.

4. **O(n log n)** – Linearithmic time: This is common in more efficient sorting algorithms, such as quicksort or mergesort. It grows slower than O(n^2) but faster than O(n).

   o **Example**: Merge sort.

5. **O(n^2)** – Quadratic time: The algorithm's runtime grows quadratically with the input size. This happens when an algorithm has nested loops that iterate through the entire input.

   o **Example**: Bubble sort or selection sort.

6. **O(2^n)** – Exponential time: The algorithm's runtime grows exponentially as the input size increases. These algorithms are inefficient for large inputs.

      o **Example**: Brute force solutions to problems like the traveling salesman problem.

7. **O(n!)** – Factorial time: The algorithm's runtime grows at a factorial rate, often seen in problems that involve generating all permutations of a set.

      o **Example**: Solving the traveling salesman problem by checking all possible paths.

Examples: Comparing Simple Algorithms

Let's take a look at two simple algorithms to compare their time complexities: **Linear Search** and **Binary Search**.

1. **Linear Search (O(n))**:

      o **Description**: Linear search scans each element in an array or list one by one until it finds the target element.

      o **Time Complexity**: The algorithm has to check every element, so in the worst case, it will take O(n) time, where n is the number of elements in the list.

      o **Example**:

cpp

```
int linearSearch(int arr[], int
size, int target) {
    for (int i = 0; i < size; i++) {
```

31

```
        if (arr[i] == target) {
            return i;   // Found the
element
        }
    }
    return -1;   // Element not found
}
```

- **Worst-case scenario**: If the target element is not found, the algorithm will have to check every element in the array.

2. **Binary Search (O(log n))**:
   o **Description**: Binary search works on sorted arrays. It divides the array in half with each step, checking if the target element is in the left or right half. It continues halving the search space until the element is found or the space is exhausted.
   o **Time Complexity**: Binary search reduces the search space by half each time, so its time complexity is O(log n).
   o **Example**:

cpp

```
int binarySearch(int arr[], int
size, int target) {
    int left = 0, right = size - 1;
    while (left <= right) {
```

```cpp
        int mid = left + (right -
left) / 2;
        if (arr[mid] == target) {
            return mid;  // Found the
element
        }
        if (arr[mid] < target) {
            left = mid + 1;    //
Search the right half
        } else {
            right = mid - 1;   //
Search the left half
        }
    }
    return -1;  // Element not found
}
```

- **Worst-case scenario**: In the worst case, binary search will only have to perform log(n) comparisons.

Comparison:

- **Linear Search**: If you have 1,000 elements, linear search might need up to 1,000 checks.
- **Binary Search**: On the other hand, binary search, even for 1,000 elements, would only require around 10 comparisons (log2(1000) ≈ 10).

Clearly, binary search is much more efficient than linear search, especially as the size of the array grows.

Real-World Scenarios Explaining the Importance of Optimization

1. **Processing Large Data Sets**: In today's world, we deal with enormous amounts of data, especially in fields like machine learning, finance, and web analytics. Consider a scenario where you need to sort and search through millions of records. An inefficient algorithm like **bubble sort** (O(n^2)) would take an unacceptably long time, whereas an optimized algorithm like **merge sort** (O(n log n)) can handle the same task much faster.

2. **Real-Time Systems**: In systems where **real-time processing** is crucial (e.g., self-driving cars or financial trading algorithms), the importance of optimized algorithms cannot be overstated. A slight delay in processing could lead to catastrophic results, such as missed opportunities or incorrect decisions. Here, algorithms that can run in **O(log n)** or **O(1)** time are preferred because they ensure timely responses, even as the size of the input data grows.

3. **Memory Usage in Embedded Systems**: For **embedded systems** (e.g., devices with limited memory), it is not just about speed but also memory usage. Algorithms that have lower **space complexity** are necessary to fit within the device's memory limits. For example, using an efficient

linked list instead of an array might help in situations where memory allocation needs to be dynamic and the size of the data is not fixed.

4. **Web Applications and APIs**: Web applications must often handle a large number of user requests at once. Consider an API that fetches user data. If the API uses a naive algorithm with high time complexity, it might result in slow response times, affecting user experience. Optimizing the backend logic with algorithms that have better time complexity can ensure that the application scales well, even with increasing traffic.

Conclusion

Understanding **Big O notation** and its implications on time and space complexity is crucial for developing efficient algorithms. As we've seen, the choice of algorithm can drastically affect performance, especially when processing large datasets or building applications that require fast responses. This chapter has introduced you to Big O notation, explained how to analyze algorithms, and demonstrated the importance of optimization in real-world scenarios. Moving forward, you'll be equipped with the knowledge to write more efficient C++ code as you tackle data structures and algorithms.

CHAPTER 4

ARRAYS – BASICS AND IMPLEMENTATION

In this chapter, we will explore **arrays**, one of the most fundamental and widely used data structures in C++. Arrays are essential for storing multiple values of the same type in a contiguous memory block, and they are used in various applications, from simple programs to complex systems. We will cover single-dimensional and multi-dimensional arrays, array operations, and real-world use cases such as game boards and image processing.

Introduction to Arrays in C++

An **array** is a data structure that stores a fixed-size sequence of elements of the same data type. It allows you to access each element by its index or position in the array. Arrays in C++ are zero-based, meaning the first element of an array is at index 0.

Here's a basic example of how to declare an array in C++:

cpp

```cpp
int arr[5]; // Declaration of an array of 5
integers
```

In this case, the array `arr` can store 5 integers. Each element in the array can be accessed using its index, starting from 0. For example, `arr[0]` will access the first element, `arr[1]` will access the second element, and so on.

Arrays can be initialized in two ways:

1. **Static Initialization**: When you know the values beforehand.

   cpp

   ```cpp
   int arr[5] = {1, 2, 3, 4, 5}; // Array
   with 5 values initialized
   ```

2. **Dynamic Initialization**: You can initialize values later.

   cpp

   ```cpp
   int arr[5];
   arr[0] = 10; // Initializing the first
   element
   arr[1] = 20; // Initializing the second
   element
   ```

Single-Dimensional and Multi-Dimensional Arrays

Single-Dimensional Arrays: A single-dimensional array is a list of elements, where each element is accessed by its index. It is the most basic form of array and is often used for storing a list of related data.

Example:

cpp

```cpp
int numbers[5] = {10, 20, 30, 40, 50};
```

Here, the `numbers` array stores five integers, and we can access each element using its index: `numbers[0]`, `numbers[1]`, etc.

Multi-Dimensional Arrays: A multi-dimensional array is an array of arrays, where each element is itself an array. The most common type of multi-dimensional array is the **2D array**, which can be thought of as a grid (like a table or a matrix).

Example of a 2D Array:

cpp

```cpp
int matrix[3][3] = {
    {1, 2, 3},
    {4, 5, 6},
    {7, 8, 9}
```

```
};
```

In this case, `matrix` is a 2D array (a 3x3 matrix), and each element can be accessed by two indices: `matrix[0][0]` for the element at the first row and first column, `matrix[2][2]` for the element in the third row and third column, and so on.

You can also use **loops** to traverse and manipulate multi-dimensional arrays:

cpp

```cpp
for (int i = 0; i < 3; i++) {
    for (int j = 0; j < 3; j++) {
        cout << matrix[i][j] << " ";
    }
    cout << endl;
}
```

Array Operations: Insertion, Deletion, and Traversal

1. **Insertion**: Insertion in an array involves placing an element at a specific position. Arrays in C++ have a fixed size, so you need to ensure that the array has enough space to accommodate the new element.

   Example (inserting an element at a specific position in an array):

   cpp

```cpp
void insert(int arr[], int &size, int
element, int position) {
    if (position >= size) {
        cout << "Position out of bounds."
<< endl;
        return;
    }
    for (int i = size; i > position; i--)
{
        arr[i] = arr[i - 1];    // Shift
elements to the right
    }
    arr[position] = element;    // Insert
element
    size++;  // Increment size
}
```

In this example, insert shifts elements to the right to make space for the new element at the specified position.

2. **Deletion**: Deletion in an array involves removing an element from a specified position and shifting the remaining elements to fill the gap.

Example (deleting an element from a specific position):

cpp

```cpp
void deleteElement(int arr[], int &size,
int position) {
    if (position >= size) {
        cout << "Position out of bounds."
<< endl;
        return;
    }
    for (int i = position; i < size - 1;
i++) {
        arr[i] = arr[i + 1];    // Shift
elements to the left
    }
    size--;   // Decrease the size of the
array
}
```

3. **Traversal**: Traversing an array involves accessing each element, usually with a loop, to perform some operation on it. This operation could be printing, modifying, or calculating something based on the elements.

Example (traversing an array):

cpp

```cpp
void traverse(int arr[], int size) {
    for (int i = 0; i < size; i++) {
        cout << arr[i] << " ";
    }
```

41

```
        cout << endl;
    }
```

Real-World Use Case: Implementing a Matrix for Game Boards or Image Processing

One of the most common real-world applications of arrays is in **game boards** or **image processing**, where data is represented in a grid-like structure.

Example 1: Implementing a Game Board

Imagine you are building a **tic-tac-toe** game. You can use a 2D array to represent the game board, where each element in the array corresponds to a cell on the board.

Code Example:

cpp

```cpp
#include <iostream>
using namespace std;

void printBoard(char board[3][3]) {
    for (int i = 0; i < 3; i++) {
        for (int j = 0; j < 3; j++) {
            cout << board[i][j] << " ";
        }
        cout << endl;
    }
}
```

```
int main() {
    char board[3][3] = {{' ', ' ', ' '}, {' ', '
', ' '}, {' ', ' ', ' '}};

    printBoard(board);  // Print the empty board

    // Example: Player 'X' makes a move
    board[0][0] = 'X';
    printBoard(board);   // Print the updated
board after the move

    return 0;
}
```

In this example, the board is a 3x3 grid, and you can update the cells by placing 'X' or 'O' to represent player moves.

Example   2:   Image   Processing
Arrays are also crucial in **image processing**, where images are often represented as matrices. Each pixel in an image is represented by an element in a 2D array. In grayscale images, each pixel can be represented by a single value (e.g., 0 for black, 255 for white), while in colored images, each pixel can be represented by an array of three values (for red, green, and blue components).

For instance, let's represent a simple grayscale image as a matrix and print it out:

cpp

```cpp
#include <iostream>
using namespace std;

void printImage(int image[3][3]) {
    for (int i = 0; i < 3; i++) {
        for (int j = 0; j < 3; j++) {
            cout << image[i][j] << " ";
        }
        cout << endl;
    }
}

int main() {
    int image[3][3] = {{0, 255, 0}, {255, 255, 255}, {0, 0, 0}};

    printImage(image);   // Print the grayscale image matrix

    return 0;
}
```

In this example, each element in the 2D array represents a pixel in a grayscale image, with 0 representing black and 255 representing white.

Conclusion

In this chapter, you've learned about arrays in C++, starting from their basic structure to their implementation in both single-dimensional and multi-dimensional formats. We covered the key operations on arrays—**insertion**, **deletion**, and **traversal**—and explored real-world use cases such as implementing game boards and processing images. Arrays are versatile and essential for handling collections of data in a wide range of applications, setting the foundation for more advanced data structures in subsequent chapters.

CHAPTER 5

STRINGS – REPRESENTATION AND ALGORITHMS

In this chapter, we'll explore **strings** in C++ — one of the most commonly used data types for handling text. We will discuss how strings are represented, various algorithms for manipulating strings (such as searching for substrings), and how to implement string-based features like those in a text editor search function. Additionally, we'll look at some of the powerful string handling features available in C++'s standard library.

Understanding String Handling in C++

A **string** in C++ is essentially an array of characters, with each character stored in a contiguous block of memory. C++ provides two main ways to represent and work with strings:

1. **C-Style Strings** (Character arrays): In older C++ programs, strings are often represented as arrays of characters, terminated by a special null character ('\0') to indicate the end of the string.

   Example of a C-style string:

```
cpp
```

```cpp
char str[] = "Hello, world!";
```

Here, `str` is an array of characters that stores the string "Hello, world!" and ends with a null character `'\0'`.

2. **C++ Standard Library Strings** (`std::string`): The **std::string** class, provided by C++'s Standard Library, offers a higher-level and more convenient way to work with strings. Unlike C-style strings, `std::string` automatically manages memory and provides many useful functions to manipulate text.

Example of a C++ string:

```
cpp
```

```cpp
#include <iostream>
#include <string>
using namespace std;

int main() {
    string str = "Hello, world!";
    cout << str << endl;   // Output the string
    return 0;
}
```

std::string is dynamic, so it can grow or shrink as needed, and it handles memory management automatically. It also provides a wide range of member functions that make string manipulation much simpler.

String Manipulation Algorithms

String manipulation is a fundamental skill in C++ programming. Below are some of the common algorithms used to manipulate and process strings.

1. **Substring Search**: One of the most common string operations is searching for a substring within a string. C++ provides several ways to perform substring search, but the most straightforward way is using the **find()** function of the std::string class.

   Example of substring search using find():

   cpp

   ```cpp
   #include <iostream>
   #include <string>
   using namespace std;

   int main() {
       string str = "The quick brown fox";
       string target = "quick";
   ```

```cpp
    size_t found = str.find(target);
    if (found != string::npos) {
        cout << "'" << target << "' found
at position " << found << endl;
    } else {
        cout << "'" << target << "' not
found" << endl;
    }
    return 0;
}
```

In this example, the `find()` function returns the index of the first occurrence of the substring `"quick"` within the string `"The quick brown fox"`. If the substring is not found, it returns `string::npos`.

2. **String Concatenation**: Concatenating (joining) strings is another common operation. The + operator or the **append()** function can be used to concatenate strings in C++.

    Example of string concatenation:

    cpp

```cpp
string str1 = "Hello, ";
string str2 = "world!";
string result = str1 + str2;    //
Concatenating two strings
```

49

```cpp
cout << result << endl;   // Output: "Hello,
world!"
```

Alternatively, you can use the append() method:

cpp

```cpp
str1.append(str2);   // Append str2 to str1
cout << str1 << endl;   // Output: "Hello,
world!"
```

3. **String Reversal**: Reversing a string is another useful string manipulation task. You can use the **reverse()** function from the C++ standard library to reverse a string in-place.

    Example of reversing a string:

    cpp

    ```cpp
    #include <algorithm>
    string str = "Hello";
    reverse(str.begin(),   str.end());   //
    Reverse the string
    cout << str << endl;   // Output: "olleH"
    ```

4. **String Comparison**: C++ allows easy comparison of strings using comparison operators (==, <, >, etc.) or the **compare()** function.

Example of string comparison:

cpp

```cpp
string str1 = "apple";
string str2 = "banana";
if (str1.compare(str2) == 0) {
    cout << "Strings are equal." << endl;
} else {
    cout << "Strings are not equal." << endl;
}
```

Use Case: Implementing a Text Editor Search Feature

One of the most common uses for string manipulation is implementing search features in applications such as **text editors**. Let's consider implementing a basic search function that allows users to search for a substring within a larger text (similar to the "Find" feature in many text editors).

Here's a simple C++ program that implements a basic **text search** function:

Example: Text search in a simple text editor:

cpp

```cpp
#include <iostream>
#include <string>
```

```cpp
using namespace std;

void searchText(const string &text, const string
&searchTerm) {
    size_t pos = text.find(searchTerm);     //
Search for the term in the text
    if (pos != string::npos) {
        cout << "Found '" << searchTerm << "' at
position: " << pos << endl;
    } else {
        cout << "'" << searchTerm << "' not
found!" << endl;
    }
}

int main() {
    string text = "This is a simple text editor.
Find the word 'text'.";
    string searchTerm = "text";

    searchText(text, searchTerm);     // Call the
search function

    return 0;
}
```

Explanation:

- The program defines a function `searchText` that takes two arguments: the text to search and the search term.
- It uses the `find()` function to search for the `searchTerm` within the `text`.
- If the term is found, it prints the position of the first occurrence of the substring. Otherwise, it informs the user that the term was not found.

This is a simple implementation of a search feature that could be expanded to include features like **case-insensitive search**, **highlighting matching text**, or **searching for multiple occurrences**.

Exploring C++ Standard Library Functions for String Handling

The **C++ Standard Library** offers a rich set of built-in functions to work with strings. Here are a few commonly used string functions from the `std::string` class:

1. **length() or size()**: Returns the length of the string (number of characters).

cpp

```cpp
string str = "Hello";
cout << "Length: " << str.length() << endl;
// Output: 5
```

2. **substr()**: Returns a substring from a given string, starting at a specific index and optionally specifying the length of the substring.

cpp

```cpp
string str = "Hello, world!";
string sub = str.substr(7, 5);  // Extracts
"world"
cout << sub << endl;
```

3. **c_str()**: Converts a std::string to a C-style string (const char*).

cpp

```cpp
string str = "Hello";
const char* cstr = str.c_str();
cout << cstr << endl;  // Output: "Hello"
```

4. **erase()**: Removes a portion of the string starting from a given position.

cpp

```cpp
string str = "Hello, world!";
str.erase(5, 7);  // Removes ", world"
cout << str << endl;  // Output: "Hello"
```

5. **replace()**: Replaces part of the string with another substring.

cpp

```
string str = "Hello, world!";
str.replace(7, 5, "C++");    // Replace
"world" with "C++"
cout << str << endl;  // Output: "Hello,
C++!"
```

Conclusion

In this chapter, you've learned about string handling in C++, covering both **C-style strings** and the more modern **std::string** class. We explored key string manipulation algorithms, including substring search, string concatenation, and reversal. Additionally, we built a simple **text editor search feature** and highlighted powerful string functions provided by the C++ Standard Library. Mastering these techniques will provide you with the tools necessary to work effectively with text data in your C++ programs.

CHAPTER 6

LINKED LISTS – CONCEPT AND IMPLEMENTATION

In this chapter, we will explore **linked lists**, a fundamental data structure that allows dynamic memory allocation and efficient insertion and deletion operations. We will focus on **singly linked lists** and **doubly linked lists**, explaining their structure, how to implement them, and how to traverse them. Additionally, we will explore a real-world use case of linked lists in dynamic memory management, such as in **music playlists**.

Explanation of Singly Linked Lists and Doubly Linked Lists

A **linked list** is a linear data structure where elements (called **nodes**) are stored in memory in a non-contiguous manner. Each node contains two components:

1. **Data**: The value or data stored in the node.
2. **Next/Previous Pointer**: A pointer that references the next node (in a singly linked list) or both the next and previous nodes (in a doubly linked list).

There are two main types of linked lists:

- **Singly Linked List**: In a singly linked list, each node points to the next node in the sequence, but there is no reference to the previous node. This allows traversal in one direction only.

  Structure of a singly linked list:

  css

  ```
  [Data | Next] -> [Data | Next] -> [Data |
  Next] -> NULL
  ```

- **Doubly Linked List**: In a doubly linked list, each node contains two pointers: one pointing to the next node and one pointing to the previous node. This allows traversal in both directions: forward and backward.

  Structure of a doubly linked list:

  css

  ```
  NULL <- [Prev | Data | Next] <-> [Prev |
  Data | Next] <-> [Prev | Data | Next] ->
  NULL
  ```

How to Implement and Traverse Linked Lists

1. **Singly Linked List Implementation**:

A **singly linked list** can be implemented by defining a node structure and using a pointer to traverse the list. Below is the implementation of a basic singly linked list in C++:

Node Structure:

cpp

```cpp
struct Node {
    int data;
    Node* next;
};
```

Creating and Inserting Nodes:

cpp

```cpp
#include <iostream>
using namespace std;

struct Node {
    int data;
    Node* next;
};

// Function to create a new node and insert
at the beginning
```

```cpp
void insertAtBeginning(Node*& head, int
value) {
    Node* newNode = new Node();  // Create
new node
    newNode->data = value;  // Assign data
to the node
    newNode->next = head;  // Point the new
node to the current head
    head = newNode;  // Make the new node
the new head
}

// Function to traverse and print the
linked list
void traverse(Node* head) {
    Node* current = head;
    while (current != nullptr) {
        cout << current->data << " ";
        current = current->next;
    }
    cout << endl;
}

int main() {
    Node* head = nullptr;  // Initialize an
empty list
    insertAtBeginning(head, 10);
    insertAtBeginning(head, 20);
    insertAtBeginning(head, 30);
```

```cpp
    traverse(head);   // Output: 30 20 10
    return 0;
}
```

Explanation:

- o **insertAtBeginning** creates a new node, assigns the data to it, and inserts it at the beginning of the list.
- o **traverse** goes through the list starting from the head and prints the data of each node.

2. **Doubly Linked List Implementation**:

A **doubly linked list** can be implemented similarly, but with two pointers (prev and next) for each node. Here's how you can implement it:

Node Structure:

cpp

```cpp
struct Node {
    int data;
    Node* next;
    Node* prev;
};
```

Creating and Inserting Nodes:

```cpp
cpp

#include <iostream>
using namespace std;

struct Node {
    int data;
    Node* next;
    Node* prev;
};

// Function to create a new node and insert
at the beginning
void insertAtBeginning(Node*& head, int
value) {
    Node* newNode = new Node();  // Create
new node
    newNode->data = value;  // Assign data
to the node
    newNode->prev = nullptr;    // The
previous pointer is null for the first node
    newNode->next = head;  // Point the new
node to the current head

    if (head != nullptr) {  // If the list
is not empty
        head->prev = newNode;  // Set the
previous pointer of the old head
    }
```

```cpp
    head = newNode;   // Make the new node
the new head
}


// Function to traverse and print the
doubly linked list
void traverse(Node* head) {
    Node* current = head;
    while (current != nullptr) {
        cout << current->data << " ";
        current = current->next;
    }
    cout << endl;
}


int main() {
    Node* head = nullptr;  // Initialize an
empty list
    insertAtBeginning(head, 10);
    insertAtBeginning(head, 20);
    insertAtBeginning(head, 30);

    traverse(head);   // Output: 30 20 10
    return 0;
}
```

Explanation:

- o **insertAtBeginning** creates a new node and inserts it at the beginning of the doubly linked list, setting both the `next` and `prev` pointers accordingly.
- o **traverse** prints the elements of the list starting from the `head` and following the `next` pointers.

Use Case: Dynamic Memory Management in Applications Like Music Playlists

One real-world application of linked lists is in **dynamic memory management**, particularly in **music playlists**. A music playlist can be modeled as a linked list, where each song is represented by a node containing song information (e.g., title, artist, duration) and pointers to the next (and possibly previous) song in the playlist.

In this scenario:

- The playlist can grow or shrink dynamically as songs are added or removed.
- Linked lists allow efficient insertion and deletion of songs, as there is no need to resize a fixed-size array or reorganize data.

Example: Implementing a Simple Music Playlist with a Singly Linked List:

cpp

```cpp
#include <iostream>
#include <string>
using namespace std;

struct Song {
    string title;
    string artist;
    Song* next;
};

// Function to add a song to the playlist
void addSong(Song*& head, const string& title,
const string& artist) {
    Song* newSong = new Song();
    newSong->title = title;
    newSong->artist = artist;
    newSong->next = head;
    head = newSong;
}


// Function to display the playlist
void displayPlaylist(Song* head) {
    Song* current = head;
    while (current != nullptr) {
        cout << "Song: " << current->title << "
by " << current->artist << endl;
        current = current->next;
    }
```

```
}

int main() {
    Song* playlist = nullptr;

    // Adding songs to the playlist
    addSong(playlist,   "Shape   of   You",   "Ed
Sheeran");
    addSong(playlist,   "Blinding   Lights",   "The
Weeknd");
    addSong(playlist, "Levitating", "Dua Lipa");

    // Displaying the playlist
    displayPlaylist(playlist);
    return 0;
}
```

Explanation:

- **addSong** adds a song to the playlist (represented as a singly linked list) by inserting it at the beginning.
- **displayPlaylist** prints all the songs in the playlist by traversing the linked list from the head.

This example shows how a linked list can be used to represent a playlist, allowing dynamic addition of songs. You can easily extend this to remove songs, search for a song, or reorder the playlist.

Conclusion

In this chapter, we explored **linked lists** in C++ and how they differ from other data structures like arrays. We covered **singly linked lists** and **doubly linked lists**, focusing on their structure and how to implement them in C++. We also discussed a real-world use case of linked lists in **dynamic memory management**, such as in **music playlists**. Linked lists are an efficient way to manage dynamic data, providing flexibility in scenarios where the size of the data is not known in advance. With these foundations, you are now ready to implement more complex data structures in C++.

CHAPTER 7

STACKS – LAST-IN, FIRST-OUT (LIFO) STRUCTURE

In this chapter, we will delve into **stacks**, one of the most commonly used abstract data structures in computer science. Stacks operate on the principle of **Last-In, First-Out (LIFO)**, meaning the most recently added element is the first to be removed. We will cover the **applications** of stacks, how to **implement a stack** using both arrays and linked lists, and explore a **real-world application** of stacks: the **undo functionality** in text editors.

Introduction to Stacks and Their Applications

A **stack** is a linear data structure where elements are inserted and removed only from one end, called the **top**. The key operations for a stack are:

1. **Push**: Adds an element to the top of the stack.
2. **Pop**: Removes the element from the top of the stack.
3. **Peek/Top**: Retrieves the element at the top of the stack without removing it.
4. **isEmpty**: Checks whether the stack is empty.

The LIFO behavior of stacks is useful in many real-world scenarios:

- **Function Call Stack**: In programming, the system uses a stack to keep track of function calls and local variables.
- **Undo/Redo Functionality**: In applications like text editors, stacks are used to store previous states so that users can undo actions.
- **Expression Evaluation**: Stacks are used in algorithms for evaluating arithmetic expressions (infix, postfix, and prefix).

Stacks are also used in **parsing** algorithms, **depth-first search** in graphs, and **backtracking** problems.

Implementing a Stack Using Arrays and Linked Lists

1. **Implementing a Stack Using Arrays**

In an array-based implementation of a stack, we maintain a **fixed-size array** to store elements. We use an integer to keep track of the index of the top element.

Example: Array-based stack implementation in C++:

cpp

```
#include <iostream>
using namespace std;
```

```cpp
class Stack {
private:
    int top;
    int arr[5];   // Fixed size stack
public:
    Stack() {
        top = -1;   // Initialize the stack as empty
    }

    // Push an element onto the stack
    void push(int value) {
        if (top >= 4) {
            cout << "Stack Overflow!" << endl;
// Stack is full
        } else {
            arr[++top] = value;  // Increment top and insert value
            cout << value << " pushed onto stack" << endl;
        }
    }

    // Pop an element from the stack
    void pop() {
        if (top < 0) {
            cout << "Stack Underflow!" << endl;
// Stack is empty
```

```cpp
        } else {
            cout << arr[top--] << " popped from
stack" << endl;
        }
    }


    // Peek the top element of the stack
    void peek() {
        if (top >= 0) {
            cout <<  "Top  element  is:  "  <<
arr[top] << endl;
        } else {
            cout << "Stack is empty" << endl;
        }
    }


    // Check if the stack is empty
    bool isEmpty() {
        return top == -1;
    }
};


int main() {
    Stack s;
    s.push(10);
    s.push(20);
    s.push(30);
    s.peek();  // Output: Top element is: 30
    s.pop();   // Output: 30 popped from stack
```

```
s.pop();    // Output: 20 popped from stack
s.pop();    // Output: 10 popped from stack
s.pop();    // Output: Stack Underflow!
return 0;
}
```

Explanation:

- The `Stack` class has an array `arr` of size 5 to store the stack elements.
- The `top` variable keeps track of the top element's index.
- The `push` function adds an element to the stack, the `pop` function removes the top element, and `peek` displays the top element without removing it.
- **Overflow** and **underflow** conditions are handled by checking the `top` index.

2. **Implementing a Stack Using Linked Lists**

In a linked list-based implementation of a stack, each node of the list contains an element and a pointer to the next node. The stack operations (`push`, `pop`, `peek`) are performed on the head of the list, making them more dynamic and allowing for potentially unlimited size (limited only by memory).

Example: Linked list-based stack implementation in C++:

cpp

71

```cpp
#include <iostream>
using namespace std;

struct Node {
    int data;
    Node* next;
};

class Stack {
private:
    Node* top;
public:
    Stack() {
        top = nullptr;   // Initialize an empty stack
    }

    // Push an element onto the stack
    void push(int value) {
        Node* newNode = new Node();   // Create a new node
        newNode->data = value;
        newNode->next = top;   // Link new node to the previous top
        top = newNode;   // Make the new node the top of the stack
        cout << value << " pushed onto stack" << endl;
```

```cpp
    }

    // Pop an element from the stack
    void pop() {
        if (top == nullptr) {
            cout << "Stack Underflow!" << endl;
// Stack is empty
        } else {
            Node* temp = top;    // Save the
current top
            top = top->next;   // Move top to the
next node
            cout << temp->data << " popped from
stack" << endl;
            delete temp;   // Free memory
        }
    }

    // Peek the top element of the stack
    void peek() {
        if (top != nullptr) {
            cout << "Top element is: " << top-
>data << endl;
        } else {
            cout << "Stack is empty" << endl;
        }
    }

    // Check if the stack is empty
```

```cpp
    bool isEmpty() {
        return top == nullptr;
    }
};

int main() {
    Stack s;
    s.push(10);
    s.push(20);
    s.push(30);
    s.peek();   // Output: Top element is: 30
    s.pop();    // Output: 30 popped from stack
    s.pop();    // Output: 20 popped from stack
    s.pop();    // Output: 10 popped from stack
    s.pop();    // Output: Stack Underflow!
    return 0;
}
```

Explanation:

- The `Stack` class uses a `Node` structure to represent each element, where each node contains the `data` and a pointer to the next node.

- The `push` function creates a new node and sets it as the top of the stack.

- The `pop` function removes the top node and frees the memory.

- The `peek` function shows the data of the top node without removing it.

74

The linked list-based stack has the advantage of being dynamic, meaning the stack can grow and shrink as needed without a fixed size.

Real-World Application: Undo Functionality in Text Editors

A **common real-world use case** for stacks is in the **undo** functionality in text editors (like Microsoft Word or Google Docs). In text editors, the stack allows users to **undo** their last action, whether it's typing, deleting text, or formatting changes.

Here's how a stack can be used in this context:

- Every time a user makes a change, the previous state of the text (or action) is pushed onto a stack.
- When the user presses the "undo" button, the most recent state is popped from the stack, and the text is reverted to that state.
- The stack allows the program to **track changes** and **restore previous states**, ensuring that users can go back multiple steps in their editing process.

For example, consider a text editor that supports multiple undo operations. The program might maintain a stack of text states, where each state represents the content of the text box at a given point in time. Here's a simplified conceptual approach to implementing undo:

```cpp
cpp

class TextEditor {
private:
    Stack undoStack;  // Stack to store previous
states of the text
    string currentText;  // Current text in the
editor

public:
    TextEditor() : currentText("") {}

    // Function to type text (adds text to the
editor)
    void typeText(const string& text) {
        undoStack.push(currentText);    // Save
current state before the change
        currentText += text;  // Add new text
    }

    // Function to undo the last action
    void undo() {
        if (!undoStack.isEmpty()) {
            currentText = undoStack.top();    //
Retrieve and set the last saved state
            undoStack.pop();  // Remove the last
saved state
        } else {
            cout << "Nothing to undo" << endl;
```

```
        }
    }

    // Function to display the current text
    void displayText() {
        cout << currentText << endl;
    }
};
```

In this conceptual example:

- Each time the user types new text, the current state of the text is pushed onto the **undoStack**.
- When the user presses "undo", the most recent state is popped from the stack and set as the current text.

Conclusion

In this chapter, we explored **stacks**, a powerful and simple data structure with numerous applications in real-world scenarios. We learned how to implement stacks using both **arrays** and **linked lists** in C++, and we explored a common application: the **undo functionality in text editors**. By understanding the basic operations of stacks — **push, pop, peek,** and **isEmpty** — and seeing their use in real-world problems, you are now ready to apply stacks to various challenges in your C++ programs.

CHAPTER 8

QUEUES – FIRST-IN, FIRST-OUT (FIFO) STRUCTURE

In this chapter, we will explore **queues**, a fundamental data structure based on the principle of **First-In, First-Out (FIFO)**. A queue ensures that the first element added to the queue is the first one to be removed, much like a line of customers waiting for service. We will discuss the **applications** of queues, how to **implement queues** using arrays and linked lists, and a **real-world example** of how queues are used in **task scheduling** within operating systems.

Explanation of Queues and Their Applications

A **queue** is a linear data structure that stores elements in a sequential manner, with two main operations:

1. **Enqueue**: Adds an element to the end of the queue.
2. **Dequeue**: Removes an element from the front of the queue.

Queues are typically visualized as a line, where the **front** of the queue is where elements are dequeued (removed), and the **rear** of the queue is where new elements are enqueued (added).

Common queue operations:

- **Front**: Retrieves the element at the front of the queue without removing it.
- **isEmpty**: Checks whether the queue is empty.
- **Size**: Returns the number of elements currently in the queue.

Queues have a wide variety of applications in computer science and real-world systems:

- **Task Scheduling**: In operating systems, queues are used to manage processes or tasks that need to be executed, ensuring fair and orderly execution.
- **Printer Queue**: In a printing system, multiple print jobs can be added to a queue and processed one after another.
- **Buffering**: Queues are often used in systems that need to manage data flow, like network routers, where packets are queued before being processed.
- **Breadth-First Search (BFS)**: In graph algorithms, queues are used to explore nodes level by level.

Implementing Queues with Arrays and Linked Lists

Queues can be implemented in two primary ways: using **arrays** or **linked lists**. Each has its own set of advantages and trade-offs.

1. **Array-Based Queue Implementation**

In an array-based queue, we maintain an array and two pointers (or indices): one for the **front** of the queue and one for the **rear**. Elements are added to the rear and removed from the front. A common problem in array-based queues is **queue overflow** (when the array is full) and **queue underflow** (when the queue is empty).

Example: Array-based queue implementation in C++:

cpp

```cpp
#include <iostream>
using namespace std;

class Queue {
private:
    int front, rear, size;
    int* arr;
    int capacity;

public:
    Queue(int cap) {
        capacity = cap;
        arr = new int[capacity];
        front = 0;
        rear = -1;
        size = 0;
    }

    // Enqueue operation
```

```cpp
    void enqueue(int value) {
        if (size == capacity) {
            cout << "Queue Overflow!" << endl;
// Queue is full
        } else {
            rear = (rear + 1) % capacity;
            arr[rear] = value;
            size++;
            cout << value << " enqueued to queue"
<< endl;
        }
    }

    // Dequeue operation
    void dequeue() {
        if (size == 0) {
            cout << "Queue Underflow!" << endl;
// Queue is empty
        } else {
            cout << arr[front] << " dequeued from
queue" << endl;
            front = (front + 1) % capacity;
            size--;
        }
    }

    // Peek operation
    void peek() {
        if (size == 0) {
```

```cpp
            cout << "Queue is empty" << endl;
        } else {
            cout << "Front element is: " <<
arr[front] << endl;
        }
    }

    // Check if the queue is empty
    bool isEmpty() {
        return size == 0;
    }

    // Get the current size of the queue
    int getSize() {
        return size;
    }
};

int main() {
    Queue q(5);  // Queue with capacity 5

    q.enqueue(10);
    q.enqueue(20);
    q.enqueue(30);
    q.peek();  // Output: Front element is: 10
    q.dequeue();   // Output: 10 dequeued from
queue
    q.dequeue();   // Output: 20 dequeued from
queue
```

```
    q.dequeue();    // Output: 30 dequeued from
queue
    q.dequeue();    // Output: Queue Underflow!
    return 0;
}
```

Explanation:

- The Queue class maintains an array arr and two pointers: front (the index of the front element) and rear (the index of the last element).

- The enqueue operation adds elements to the rear, and the dequeue operation removes elements from the front.

- The use of **modulus** (% capacity) ensures that both the front and rear pointers wrap around when they reach the end of the array, creating a **circular queue**.

2. **Linked List-Based Queue Implementation**

In a linked list-based implementation, each element (node) contains both the **data** and a pointer to the **next** node. This approach allows the queue to grow dynamically, avoiding the fixed size limitation of an array-based queue.

Example: Linked list-based queue implementation in C++:

cpp

```
#include <iostream>
```

```cpp
using namespace std;

struct Node {
    int data;
    Node* next;
};

class Queue {
private:
    Node* front;
    Node* rear;

public:
    Queue() {
        front = rear = nullptr;
    }

    // Enqueue operation
    void enqueue(int value) {
        Node* newNode = new Node();
        newNode->data = value;
        newNode->next = nullptr;

        if (rear == nullptr) {
            front = rear = newNode;   // If the
queue is empty, both front and rear are the same
        } else {
            rear->next = newNode;   // Add the new
node to the end
```

```cpp
            rear = newNode;   // Update the rear
pointer
        }
        cout << value << " enqueued to queue" <<
endl;
    }


    // Dequeue operation
    void dequeue() {
        if (front == nullptr) {
            cout << "Queue Underflow!" << endl;
// Queue is empty
        } else {
            Node* temp = front;
            cout << temp->data << " dequeued from
queue" << endl;
            front = front->next;   // Move the
front pointer to the next node
            if (front == nullptr) {
                rear = nullptr;   // If the queue
is empty, set rear to nullptr
            }
            delete temp;   // Free the memory of
the dequeued node
        }
    }


    // Peek operation
    void peek() {
```

```cpp
        if (front != nullptr) {
            cout << "Front element is: " <<
front->data << endl;
        } else {
            cout << "Queue is empty" << endl;
        }
    }

    // Check if the queue is empty
    bool isEmpty() {
        return front == nullptr;
    }
};

int main() {
    Queue q;

    q.enqueue(10);
    q.enqueue(20);
    q.enqueue(30);
    q.peek();    // Output: Front element is: 10
    q.dequeue();    // Output: 10 dequeued from
queue
    q.dequeue();    // Output: 20 dequeued from
queue
    q.dequeue();    // Output: 30 dequeued from
queue
    q.dequeue();    // Output: Queue Underflow!
    return 0;
```

}

Explanation:

- The `Queue` class uses a linked list with nodes (`Node` structure) that store the data and a pointer to the next node.
- The `enqueue` operation adds elements to the rear of the queue, while the `dequeue` operation removes elements from the front.
- Unlike the array-based queue, there is no fixed size, and the queue grows dynamically as elements are added.

Real-World Example: Task Scheduling in Operating Systems

One real-world application of a queue is **task scheduling** in **operating systems**. In an operating system, processes or tasks that need to be executed are typically added to a queue. The operating system uses the queue to manage the execution of tasks in a fair and orderly manner, ensuring that tasks are processed in the order they arrive (FIFO).

In task scheduling, the operating system maintains a queue of tasks that are ready to be executed. When a task is completed, it is removed from the front of the queue, and the next task is processed. This ensures that the system runs efficiently and avoids starvation, where tasks could potentially never get executed.

Here's a simple conceptual example of how a queue can be used to manage tasks in an operating system:

cpp

```cpp
#include <iostream>
#include <queue>
#include <string>
using namespace std;

class Task {
public:
    string taskName;
    Task(string name) : taskName(name) {}
};

int main() {
    queue<Task> taskQueue;

    // Adding tasks to the queue
    taskQueue.push(Task("Task 1"));
    taskQueue.push(Task("Task 2"));
    taskQueue.push(Task("Task 3"));

    // Processing tasks
    while (!taskQueue.empty()) {
        cout      <<      "Processing      "      <<
taskQueue.front().taskName << endl;
```

88

```
        taskQueue.pop();  // Remove the processed
task
    }

    return 0;
}
```

Explanation:

- This example simulates an operating system task scheduler. The tasks are added to the `taskQueue` using `push()`.
- The tasks are processed by repeatedly calling `front()` to retrieve the next task and `pop()` to remove it from the queue.

This simple approach ensures that tasks are executed in the order they are received, demonstrating the FIFO nature of queues in real-world systems.

Conclusion

In this chapter, we explored **queues**, a crucial data structure that follows the **First-In, First-Out (FIFO)** principle. We learned how to implement queues using both **arrays** and **linked lists**, covering essential operations like **enqueue, dequeue, peek**, and **isEmpty**. Additionally, we discussed a **real-world application** of queues in **task scheduling** within operating systems, illustrating how this data structure is used to manage processes and ensure fair task execution. With this knowledge, you are now ready to apply queues to a wide variety of problems and use cases in your C++ programs.

CHAPTER 9

DEQUES AND CIRCULAR QUEUES

In this chapter, we will dive into two specialized types of queues: **double-ended queues (deques)** and **circular queues**. We will explore their structures, advantages, and how they differ from standard queues. Additionally, we will examine a real-world use case of **buffer management in video streaming** where these data structures can be effectively applied.

Understanding Double-Ended Queues (Deques)

A **double-ended queue**, or **deque**, is a linear data structure that allows elements to be added and removed from both ends — the **front** and the **rear**. This makes deques more versatile than standard queues, which only allow operations at the front and rear.

A deque supports the following operations:

- **push_front**: Adds an element to the front of the deque.
- **push_back**: Adds an element to the rear of the deque.
- **pop_front**: Removes an element from the front of the deque.

- **pop_back**: Removes an element from the rear of the deque.
- **front**: Retrieves the front element.
- **back**: Retrieves the rear element.

Advantages of Deques:

- Deques allow **efficient insertions and deletions** at both ends of the data structure.
- They are ideal when you need to **manage elements in both directions** in a scenario, such as in some **queue-based algorithms**.

Example: Deque implementation using C++ Standard Library: C++ provides a built-in **deque** container in the **Standard Template Library (STL)**. Below is a simple example using the deque from STL.

cpp

```cpp
#include <iostream>
#include <deque>
using namespace std;

int main() {
    deque<int> d;

    // Adding elements to both ends of the deque
```

```cpp
    d.push_back(10);   // Add to rear
    d.push_front(20);  // Add to front
    d.push_back(30);   // Add to rear

    // Displaying elements of deque
    cout << "Deque contents: ";
    for (int elem : d) {
        cout << elem << " ";   // Output: 20 10 30
    }
    cout << endl;

    // Removing elements from both ends of the
deque
    d.pop_front();   // Removes 20 from the front
    d.pop_back();    // Removes 30 from the rear

    // Displaying the deque after pop operations
    cout << "Deque after pop operations: ";
    for (int elem : d) {
        cout << elem << " ";   // Output: 10
    }
    cout << endl;

    return 0;
}
```

Explanation:

93

- **push_back** and **push_front** allow insertion at both ends of the deque.
- **pop_back** and **pop_front** remove elements from the respective ends.
- The deque provides an easy way to manage elements from both ends efficiently.

Circular Queues and Their Advantages

A **circular queue** is a more specialized form of a queue where the last position is connected to the first position in the array (hence forming a circle). This allows the queue to utilize available space more efficiently.

In a standard queue, once the rear pointer reaches the end of the array, **no more elements** can be added, even if there is space at the front of the array after dequeue operations. A circular queue addresses this problem by making the rear pointer "wrap around" to the front when space becomes available.

Key Characteristics of Circular Queues:

- **Fixed size**: Circular queues are implemented using arrays of fixed size, which can lead to more efficient memory usage.
- **Circular behavior**: The rear pointer wraps around to the front when it reaches the end of the array, making use of all available space.

94

Circular Queue Operations:

1. **Enqueue**: Adds an element to the rear of the queue. If the queue is full (rear is at the last index and front is at the first index), it wraps around.
2. **Dequeue**: Removes an element from the front of the queue and advances the front pointer.
3. **Front**: Returns the element at the front of the queue.
4. **Rear**: Returns the element at the rear of the queue.

Advantages of Circular Queues:

- **Space efficiency**: It uses the available space in the array more effectively by allowing wrapping of the front and rear pointers.
- **Continuous operation**: It avoids wasting space as in a normal queue, where elements are dequeued from the front but unused space remains at the rear.

Example: Circular queue implementation in C++:

cpp

```cpp
#include <iostream>
using namespace std;

class CircularQueue {
private:
    int* arr;
```

```cpp
    int front, rear, size;
    int capacity;

public:
    CircularQueue(int cap) {
        capacity = cap;
        arr = new int[capacity];
        front = -1;
        rear = -1;
        size = 0;
    }

    // Enqueue operation
    void enqueue(int value) {
        if (size == capacity) {
            cout << "Queue Overflow!" << endl;
// Queue is full
        } else {
            if (front == -1) {
                front = 0;   // First element to
be added
            }
            rear = (rear + 1) % capacity;    //
Circular increment
            arr[rear] = value;
            size++;
            cout << value << " enqueued to queue"
<< endl;
        }
```

```cpp
    }

    // Dequeue operation
    void dequeue() {
        if (size == 0) {
            cout << "Queue Underflow!" << endl;
// Queue is empty
        } else {
            cout << arr[front] << " dequeued from
queue" << endl;
            front = (front + 1) % capacity;   //
Circular increment
            size--;
        }
    }

    // Peek operation
    void peek() {
        if (size == 0) {
            cout << "Queue is empty" << endl;
        } else {
            cout << "Front element is: " <<
arr[front] << endl;
        }
    }

    // Check if the queue is empty
    bool isEmpty() {
        return size == 0;
```

```cpp
    }

    // Get the current size of the queue
    int getSize() {
        return size;
    }
};

int main() {
    CircularQueue q(5);   // Circular queue with
capacity 5

    q.enqueue(10);
    q.enqueue(20);
    q.enqueue(30);
    q.peek();   // Output: Front element is: 10
    q.dequeue();    // Output: 10 dequeued from
queue
    q.dequeue();    // Output: 20 dequeued from
queue
    q.dequeue();    // Output: 30 dequeued from
queue
    q.dequeue();   // Output: Queue Underflow!
    return 0;
}
```

Explanation:

- The `CircularQueue` class uses an array `arr` and two pointers (`front` and `rear`) to implement the queue.

- The **modulus operator** (`% capacity`) is used to wrap around the rear and front pointers when they reach the end of the array, making the queue circular.

- The `enqueue` and `dequeue` operations are modified to handle the circular behavior efficiently.

Real-World Example: Buffer Management in Video Streaming

One real-world use case of **circular queues** is in **buffer management for video streaming**. In a video streaming application, data (such as video frames or audio packets) is received continuously and needs to be buffered before being processed. The buffer operates as a **circular queue**, where video frames are stored in the buffer and processed in sequence.

For example, as video frames are downloaded from a server, they are added to the buffer (enqueue). Once a frame is processed and displayed to the user, it is removed from the buffer (dequeue). The circular nature of the buffer ensures that it doesn't waste memory space, as the rear pointer wraps around to the front when space becomes available.

Why a Circular Queue?

- Video streaming often requires **real-time data processing**. As new video frames are received, the system needs to ensure there is always space in the buffer for the incoming data while also processing the old frames.

- Using a circular queue allows the buffer to operate continuously, making optimal use of memory without overflow, as new frames can overwrite older, processed frames.

Conclusion

In this chapter, we explored two advanced types of queues: **double-ended queues (deques)** and **circular queues**. Deques provide flexibility with insertion and deletion at both ends, while circular queues allow for efficient use of memory by wrapping around the array. We implemented both types of queues in C++ and examined their real-world application in **buffer management for video streaming**. Understanding these specialized queue structures equips you with powerful tools to solve more complex problems in your programs.

CHAPTER 10

HASH TABLES – EFFICIENT SEARCHING AND INSERTION

In this chapter, we will explore **hash tables**, a powerful and efficient data structure for searching, insertion, and deletion operations. Hash tables are particularly useful for scenarios where fast access to data is needed. We will cover the **concept of hash functions**, how to handle **hash collisions**, and how to **implement hash tables** in C++. Additionally, we will explore a **real-world use case** of hash tables: implementing a **caching system for web applications**.

Concept of Hash Functions and Hash Collisions

A **hash table** is a data structure that stores key-value pairs, and it uses a **hash function** to compute an index (hash) into an array of buckets or slots, from which the desired value can be found.

- **Hash Function**: A hash function takes a key (which can be a string, integer, etc.) and returns an integer, which is used as an index in the hash table. The hash function needs to distribute keys evenly across the table to avoid clustering, ensuring efficient lookup, insertion, and deletion.

Example of a simple hash function:

cpp

```cpp
int simpleHash(int key, int tableSize) {
    return key % tableSize;    // Simple
modulo-based hash function
}
```

This hash function computes the index by dividing the key by the table size and taking the remainder.

- **Hash Collisions**: A **hash collision** occurs when two different keys generate the same index. Collisions are inevitable, especially when the number of keys exceeds the number of available slots in the hash table.

Handling Collisions: There are several strategies to handle collisions:

1. **Chaining**: Each table index holds a linked list (or another collection) of all entries that hash to the same index.
2. **Open Addressing**: When a collision occurs, the algorithm searches for the next available slot within the table (e.g., linear probing, quadratic probing, or double hashing).

Let's dive deeper into how we can implement a hash table in C++ using chaining.

Implementing Hash Tables in C++

We will implement a basic hash table using **separate chaining**, where each bucket in the hash table holds a linked list of elements that hash to the same index.

1. **Node Structure**: Each node in the linked list will store a **key-value pair**.

    cpp

    ```cpp
    struct Node {
        int key;
        int value;
        Node* next;   // Pointer to the next
    node in the list
    };
    ```

2. **Hash Table Implementation**: We will define a hash table class that uses an array of pointers to the head of linked lists for separate chaining.

    Code Example: Hash Table with Separate Chaining in C++:

    cpp

```cpp
#include <iostream>
using namespace std;

class HashTable {
private:
    static const int tableSize = 10;
    Node* table[tableSize];   // Array of
pointers to linked lists

public:
    HashTable() {
        // Initialize each element of the
table to nullptr
        for (int i = 0; i < tableSize; i++)
{
            table[i] = nullptr;
        }
    }

    // Hash function to compute index from
key
    int hash(int key) {
        return key % tableSize;  // Simple
modulo-based hash function
    }

    // Insert key-value pair into the hash
table
```

```cpp
    void insert(int key, int value) {
        int index = hash(key);
        Node* newNode = new Node();
        newNode->key = key;
        newNode->value = value;
        newNode->next = table[index];   // Insert at the beginning of the list
        table[index] = newNode;
        cout << "Inserted (" << key << ", " << value << ") at index " << index << endl;
    }

    // Search for a value by key in the hash table
    int search(int key) {
        int index = hash(key);
        Node* current = table[index];
        while (current != nullptr) {
            if (current->key == key) {
                return current->value;   // Found the value
            }
            current = current->next;
        }
        return -1;   // Not found
    }
```

```cpp
        // Remove a key-value pair from the
hash table
    void remove(int key) {
        int index = hash(key);
        Node* current = table[index];
        Node* prev = nullptr;

        while (current != nullptr &&
current->key != key) {
            prev = current;
            current = current->next;
        }

        if (current == nullptr) {
            cout << "Key not found!" <<
endl;
            return;
        }

        if (prev == nullptr) {  // Removing
the first node
            table[index] = current->next;
        } else {
            prev->next = current->next;
// Remove the node from the list
        }
        delete current;
        cout << "Removed key " << key <<
endl;
```

```
    }
};

int main() {
    HashTable ht;

    ht.insert(5, 100);
    ht.insert(15, 200);
    ht.insert(25, 300);

    cout << "Value for key 15: " <<
ht.search(15) << endl;   // Output: 200

    ht.remove(15);   // Remove key 15

    cout << "Value for key 15: " <<
ht.search(15) << endl;   // Output: -1 (not
found)

    return 0;
}
```

Explanation:

- The **hash** function computes the index for the key.
- **insert** adds a key-value pair to the hash table using separate chaining (by inserting at the head of the linked list at the computed index).

- **search** checks whether a key exists in the hash table by traversing the linked list at the computed index.
- **remove** deletes a key-value pair by removing the corresponding node from the linked list.

Use Case: Implementing a Caching System for Web Applications

A **caching system** stores frequently accessed data in memory for faster retrieval, reducing the need to query a slower data source (e.g., a database). Hash tables are commonly used for implementing caches because of their fast look-up times.

In a web application, caching can be used to store the results of expensive queries or computations. The cache stores the data with a unique key, allowing for quick access on subsequent requests.

Example: Implementing a simple caching system using a hash table:

1. **Use Case**: Suppose we are building a web application where the results of a database query (e.g., user profile information) are cached in memory for quicker access.
2. **Hash Table as a Cache**: The keys in the hash table could be **user IDs**, and the values could be the **user profile data**. Each time the application needs to retrieve a user's profile, it first checks if the data is available in the cache (the hash table). If the data is not found, the application

fetches it from the database and stores it in the cache for future use.

Here's how the caching system can be implemented with a hash table:

cpp

```cpp
#include <iostream>
#include <unordered_map>
using namespace std;

class Cache {
private:
    unordered_map<int, string> cache;    // Key:
userID, Value: user profile

public:
    // Add or update a user profile in the cache
    void    store(int    userID,    const    string&
profileData) {
        cache[userID] = profileData;
        cout << "Stored profile data for user "
<< userID << endl;
    }

    // Retrieve user profile from the cache
    string get(int userID) {
        if (cache.find(userID) != cache.end()) {
```

```cpp
            cout << "Cache hit for user " <<
userID << endl;
            return cache[userID];    // Return
cached data
        } else {
            cout << "Cache miss for user " <<
userID << endl;
            return "";  // Return empty string if
not found
        }
    }
};

int main() {
    Cache userCache;

    // Storing user profiles
    userCache.store(1, "User 1: John Doe");
    userCache.store(2, "User 2: Jane Smith");

    // Retrieving user profiles
    cout << userCache.get(1) << endl;   // Cache
hit
    cout << userCache.get(3) << endl;   // Cache
miss

    return 0;
}
```

Explanation:

- The **Cache** class uses an `unordered_map` (which is implemented using a hash table) to store user profile data.
- The **store** method adds user profile data to the cache, and the **get** method retrieves data from the cache. If the data is not found, it returns an empty string and a cache miss message.

In this simple example, the **user profile** is retrieved from the cache if available. If not, the system would typically fetch it from a database or another data source. Caching improves performance by reducing the number of database queries.

Conclusion

In this chapter, we explored **hash tables**, a data structure that allows for efficient searching and insertion through the use of **hash functions**. We implemented hash tables in C++ with **separate chaining** to handle hash collisions. Additionally, we discussed a real-world use case of hash tables in **caching systems** for web applications, which enables faster data retrieval by storing frequently accessed data in memory. By understanding the principles of hash tables, you can now apply them to optimize performance in various applications, from caching to more complex systems requiring fast data access.

111

CHAPTER 11

TREES – BASICS AND TRAVERSAL ALGORITHMS

In this chapter, we will explore **trees**, a powerful and versatile data structure that is widely used in computer science for organizing data in a hierarchical manner. We will cover the basics of trees, including **binary trees, AVL trees**, and **B-trees**, and discuss tree traversal algorithms such as **pre-order, in-order**, and **post-order**. Additionally, we will examine a **real-world application** of trees in **representing hierarchical file systems**.

Introduction to Trees (Binary Trees, AVL Trees, and B-Trees)

A **tree** is a non-linear data structure consisting of nodes, with a **root node** at the top and **children nodes** below it. Each node contains a value and references to its children (left and right, in the case of binary trees). Trees are particularly useful for representing hierarchical relationships, such as organization charts, family trees, and file systems.

1. **Binary Tree**: A **binary tree** is a tree where each node has at most **two children**, typically referred to as the **left** and **right** child. The topmost node is called the **root**, and the nodes with no children are called **leaf nodes**.

Properties of Binary Trees:

- o Each node has at most two children.
- o The left child's value is typically smaller than the parent node's value, and the right child's value is larger (this is the basic property of a **binary search tree**, or **BST**).

Example of a Binary Tree:

markdown

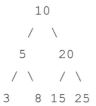

```
     10
    /  \
   5    20
  / \   / \
 3   8 15 25
```

2. **AVL Tree**: An **AVL tree** is a self-balancing **binary search tree**. In an AVL tree, the difference in heights between the left and right subtrees of any node is at most 1. If the balance factor (height difference) becomes greater than 1 or less than -1, the tree is rebalanced using **rotations**.

Properties of AVL Trees:

- o It is a **binary search tree**.

o Balancing is ensured by checking the balance factor (difference in height of left and right subtrees).

Example: In an AVL tree, a balance factor of -1, 0, or +1 is allowed at each node, ensuring that the tree remains balanced.

3. **B-Tree**: A **B-tree** is a self-balancing search tree that maintains sorted data and allows for efficient insertion, deletion, and searching. B-trees are commonly used in database indexing and file systems due to their ability to handle large amounts of data efficiently.

Properties of B-Trees:

o It is a **multi-way tree**, meaning each node can have more than two children.
o Nodes contain **multiple keys**, and the keys are kept sorted within each node.
o The tree is **balanced**, meaning the distance from the root to any leaf is the same across all paths.

B-trees are often used in database systems and file systems because they are optimized for systems that read and write large blocks of data, like hard drives or SSDs.

Tree Traversal Algorithms (Pre-order, In-order, Post-order)

Tree traversal is the process of visiting all the nodes in a tree in a specific order. Tree traversal algorithms are fundamental to working with trees, and there are different strategies to traverse a tree, each serving different purposes.

1. **Pre-order Traversal**: In **pre-order traversal**, the root node is visited first, followed by the left subtree, and then the right subtree. This traversal is useful when you need to process the root node before its children.

   Pre-order Traversal Steps:

   - o Visit the root.
   - o Traverse the left subtree.
   - o Traverse the right subtree.

   Example (Recursive Pre-order Traversal in C++):

   cpp

   ```cpp
   void preOrder(Node* root) {
       if (root != nullptr) {
           cout << root->data << " ";    //
   Visit the root
           preOrder(root->left);         //
   Traverse the left subtree
   ```

```
    preOrder(root->right);              //
Traverse the right subtree
    }
}
```

2. **In-order Traversal**: In **in-order traversal**, the left subtree is visited first, then the root node, and finally the right subtree. In-order traversal is especially useful in **binary search trees** (BSTs), as it visits the nodes in **ascending order**.

In-order Traversal Steps:

- o Traverse the left subtree.
- o Visit the root.
- o Traverse the right subtree.

Example (Recursive In-order Traversal in C++):

cpp

```
void inOrder(Node* root) {
    if (root != nullptr) {
        inOrder(root->left);              //
Traverse the left subtree
        cout << root->data << " "; // Visit
the root
        inOrder(root->right);             //
Traverse the right subtree
```

```
        }
    }
```

3. **Post-order Traversal**: In **post-order traversal**, the left subtree is visited first, followed by the right subtree, and finally the root node. This traversal is useful when you need to process the children of a node before processing the node itself, such as when deleting nodes in a tree.

Post-order Traversal Steps:

- o Traverse the left subtree.
- o Traverse the right subtree.
- o Visit the root.

Example (Recursive Post-order Traversal in C++):

cpp

```cpp
void postOrder(Node* root) {
    if (root != nullptr) {
        postOrder(root->left);         //
Traverse the left subtree
        postOrder(root->right);        //
Traverse the right subtree
        cout << root->data << " ";     //
Visit the root
    }
}
```

Real-World Application: Representing Hierarchical File Systems

One of the most important real-world applications of trees is in **file systems**, where data is organized in a hierarchical manner. The file system of an operating system typically uses a **tree structure** to represent directories and files, with the **root directory** at the top and subdirectories and files as leaf nodes.

In a **file system tree**:

- The **root node** represents the root directory.
- Each **internal node** represents a directory.
- Each **leaf node** represents a file.

For example, a file system might look like this:

markdown

```
            Root
           /    \
    Documents    Pictures
      / \          / \
  Resume.txt  Cover.jpg  Holiday.png
```

Here:

- The root directory contains two subdirectories: **Documents** and **Pictures**.

118

- The **Documents** directory contains files like **Resume.txt** and **Cover.txt**.
- The **Pictures** directory contains image files like **Cover.jpg** and **Holiday.png**.

Traversal Algorithms for File Systems:

- **Pre-order Traversal**: Visiting the root directory first, then its subdirectories, and then the files. Useful for listing all files and directories.
- **In-order Traversal**: Not commonly used in file systems but could be useful if you want to traverse subdirectories in a specific order.
- **Post-order Traversal**: Visiting the files first, then directories. Could be used when performing operations like deleting files or directories.

C++ Example: Simple File System Traversal:

cpp

```cpp
#include <iostream>
#include <vector>
#include <string>
using namespace std;

class Directory {
public:
```

```cpp
    string name;
    vector<Directory*> subdirectories;
    vector<string> files;

    Directory(string n) : name(n) {}

    void addSubdirectory(Directory* subdir) {
        subdirectories.push_back(subdir);
    }

    void addFile(string file) {
        files.push_back(file);
    }

    void traverse() {
        cout << name << " (Directory)" << endl;
        for (const string& file : files) {
            cout << "  " << file << " (File)" <<
endl;
        }
        for (Directory* subdir : subdirectories)
{
            subdir->traverse();
        }
    }
};

int main() {
    Directory root("Root");
```

Learning Data Structures: Efficient Programming with C++

```
    Directory docs("Documents");
    Directory pics("Pictures");

    docs.addFile("Resume.txt");
    docs.addFile("Cover.txt");

    pics.addFile("Cover.jpg");
    pics.addFile("Holiday.png");

    root.addSubdirectory(&docs);
    root.addSubdirectory(&pics);

    root.traverse();    // Traversing the file
system and displaying files

    return 0;
}
```

Explanation:

- The `Directory` class represents a directory in the file system, with a `name`, a list of `subdirectories`, and a list of `files`.
- The `traverse` function uses pre-order traversal to visit directories and files, printing them out.
- The file system hierarchy is represented using a tree structure, with directories as internal nodes and files as leaf nodes.

121

Conclusion

In this chapter, we explored **trees**, a powerful data structure used to represent hierarchical data. We discussed different types of trees: **binary trees**, **AVL trees**, and **B-trees**, and explored how tree traversal algorithms like **pre-order**, **in-order**, and **post-order** can be applied to process the data in these trees. We also examined a **real-world application** of trees in **representing hierarchical file systems**, showcasing how trees are used in operating systems to organize directories and files efficiently. By understanding tree structures and traversal techniques, you are now equipped to handle hierarchical data in your C++ programs.

CHAPTER 12

BINARY SEARCH TREES (BST)

In this chapter, we will delve into **Binary Search Trees (BST)**, one of the most important data structures in computer science. A BST is a specialized type of binary tree where each node has at most two children, and the values of the nodes follow a specific ordering property. We will discuss the **properties** of binary search trees, how to perform **insertion**, **deletion**, and **search** operations, and explore a **real-world application**: implementing an **address book** using a BST.

Properties and Operations of Binary Search Trees

A **Binary Search Tree (BST)** is a binary tree with the following properties:

1. **Node Value**: Each node contains a value.
2. **Left Subtree**: The value of every node in the left subtree is **less than** the value of the current node.
3. **Right Subtree**: The value of every node in the right subtree is **greater than** the value of the current node.
4. **Uniqueness**: Each node in the tree has a unique value (no duplicates allowed).

These properties make the BST a useful data structure for efficient searching, insertion, and deletion. The average time complexity of searching, inserting, and deleting elements is **O(log n)**, where n is the number of nodes in the tree. However, the time complexity can degrade to **O(n)** in the worst case (for example, when the tree becomes unbalanced and resembles a linked list).

Visual Example of a Binary Search Tree:

markdown

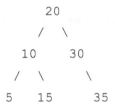

```
        20
       /  \
     10    30
    /  \     \
   5   15     35
```

In this example:

- The left subtree of the root (20) contains values less than 20 (10, 5, 15).
- The right subtree of the root contains values greater than 20 (30, 35).

Insertion, Deletion, and Search Operations

1. **Insertion in a BST**: The insertion operation places a new node with a given value in its correct position in the tree.

It starts from the root, compares the value to be inserted with the current node, and proceeds either to the left or right subtree, depending on whether the value is smaller or larger. This process continues recursively until an appropriate empty spot (null pointer) is found.

Insertion Algorithm:

- o Start at the root.
- o If the value to be inserted is less than the current node's value, move to the left child; otherwise, move to the right child.
- o When an empty spot (null pointer) is found, create a new node and place it there.

Example: Inserting 25 into the BST:

- o Start at the root (20). Since 25 > 20, move to the right child (30).
- o Since 25 < 30, move to the left child of 30, which is null.
- o Insert 25 at this position.

C++ Code for Insertion:

```cpp
struct Node {
```

```cpp
    int data;
    Node* left;
    Node* right;

    Node(int    value)    :    data(value),
left(nullptr), right(nullptr) {}
};

Node* insert(Node* root, int value) {
    if (root == nullptr) {
        return new Node(value);  // Create
a new node if the tree is empty
    }
    if (value < root->data) {
        root->left  =  insert(root->left,
value);  // Insert in the left subtree
    } else {
        root->right = insert(root->right,
value);  // Insert in the right subtree
    }
    return root;
}
```

2. **Search in a BST**: The search operation works similarly to insertion. You start at the root and move left or right based on the value you're searching for. If the value is found, you return the node; otherwise, you continue searching in the appropriate subtree.

Search Algorithm:

- o Start at the root.
- o If the value is equal to the current node, return the node.
- o If the value is smaller than the current node, search the left subtree.
- o If the value is greater than the current node, search the right subtree.

C++ Code for Search:

cpp

```cpp
Node* search(Node* root, int value) {
    if (root == nullptr || root->data ==
value) {
        return root;  // Return null if the
value is not found
    }
    if (value < root->data) {
        return search(root->left, value);
// Search in the left subtree
    }
    return search(root->right, value);  //
Search in the right subtree
}
```

3. **Deletion in a BST**: Deletion is a bit more complex since you need to maintain the BST property after the deletion. There are three possible cases to consider:

   o **Node to be deleted has no children (leaf node)**: Simply remove the node.

   o **Node to be deleted has one child**: Remove the node and link its parent to its only child.

   o **Node to be deleted has two children**: Find the **in-order successor** (smallest node in the right subtree) or **in-order predecessor** (largest node in the left subtree), replace the node to be deleted with this successor/predecessor, and then remove the successor/predecessor.

Deletion Algorithm:

   o If the node to be deleted has no children, remove it directly.

   o If the node has one child, bypass the node by linking its parent to its child.

   o If the node has two children, find the in-order successor, replace the node with the successor, and recursively delete the successor.

C++ Code for Deletion:

```
cpp
```

```cpp
Node* deleteNode(Node* root, int value) {
    if (root == nullptr) {
        return root;   // Base case: the
tree is empty
    }

    if (value < root->data) {
        root->left   =   deleteNode(root-
>left, value);   // Delete  in  the  left
subtree
    } else if (value > root->data) {
        root->right   =   deleteNode(root-
>right, value);   // Delete  in  the  right
subtree
    } else {  // Node to be deleted is found
        // Case 1: No children (leaf node)
        if (root->left == nullptr && root-
>right == nullptr) {
            delete root;
            return nullptr;
        }
        // Case 2: One child
        if (root->left == nullptr) {
            Node* temp = root->right;
            delete root;
            return temp;
        } else if (root->right == nullptr)
{
            Node* temp = root->left;
```

129

```cpp
        delete root;
        return temp;
    }


    // Case 3: Two children
    Node* temp = findMin(root->right);
// Find the in-order successor
    root->data = temp->data;      //
Replace root's value with the successor's
value
    root->right = deleteNode(root-
>right, temp->data);    // Delete the
successor
    }
    return root;
}

Node* findMin(Node* root) {
    Node* current = root;
    while (current && current->left !=
nullptr) {
        current = current->left;
    }
    return current;
}
```

Real-World Application: Implementing an Address Book

One real-world use case of a **Binary Search Tree (BST)** is implementing an **address book**. In an address book, each entry (such as a contact) has a name and associated information (such as a phone number or email address). We can use a BST to store contacts in **lexicographical order** (alphabetical order) by their names, allowing for **efficient search, insertion, and deletion** operations.

- **Insertion**: Add new contacts to the tree in alphabetical order.
- **Search**: Find a contact by name quickly.
- **Deletion**: Remove a contact by name.

Example: Implementing an address book with a BST.

cpp

```cpp
#include <iostream>
#include <string>
using namespace std;

struct Contact {
    string name;
    string phoneNumber;
    Contact* left;
    Contact* right;
```

```cpp
    Contact(string  n,  string  p)  :  name(n),
phoneNumber(p), left(nullptr), right(nullptr) {}
};

class AddressBook {
private:
    Contact* root;

public:
    AddressBook() : root(nullptr) {}

    // Insert a new contact into the address book
    void insert(string name, string phoneNumber)
{
        root   =   insertContact(root,   name,
phoneNumber);
    }

    // Search for a contact by name
    Contact* search(string name) {
        return searchContact(root, name);
    }

    // Delete a contact by name
    void remove(string name) {
        root = deleteContact(root, name);
    }
```

```cpp
    // Print the address book (in-order
traversal)
    void print() {
        printInOrder(root);
    }

private:
    Contact* insertContact(Contact* root, string
name, string phoneNumber) {
        if (root == nullptr) {
            return        new        Contact(name,
phoneNumber);
        }
        if (name < root->name) {
            root->left   =   insertContact(root-
>left, name, phoneNumber);
        } else {
            root->right   =   insertContact(root-
>right, name, phoneNumber);
        }
        return root;
    }


    Contact* searchContact(Contact* root, string
name) {
        if (root == nullptr || root->name ==
name) {
            return root;
        }
```

```cpp
        if (name < root->name) {
            return    searchContact(root->left,
name);
        }
        return searchContact(root->right, name);
    }


    Contact* deleteContact(Contact* root, string
name) {
        if (root == nullptr) {
            return root;
        }

        if (name < root->name) {
            root->left   =   deleteContact(root-
>left, name);
        } else if (name > root->name) {
            root->right   =   deleteContact(root-
>right, name);
        } else {
            if (root->left == nullptr) {
                Contact* temp = root->right;
                delete root;
                return temp;
            } else if (root->right == nullptr) {
                Contact* temp = root->left;
                delete root;
                return temp;
            }
```

```
            Contact*    temp    =    findMin(root-
>right);
            root->name = temp->name;
            root->phoneNumber       =        temp-
>phoneNumber;
            root->right   =   deleteContact(root-
>right, temp->name);
        }
        return root;
    }

    Contact* findMin(Contact* root) {
        while (root && root->left != nullptr) {
            root = root->left;
        }
        return root;
    }

    void printInOrder(Contact* root) {
        if (root != nullptr) {
            printInOrder(root->left);
            cout << root->name << ": " << root-
>phoneNumber << endl;
            printInOrder(root->right);
        }
    }
};
```

135

```cpp
int main() {
    AddressBook addressBook;

    addressBook.insert("John   Doe",   "123-456-
7890");
    addressBook.insert("Jane   Smith",   "987-654-
3210");
    addressBook.insert("Alice   Brown",   "555-555-
5555");

    cout << "Address Book:" << endl;
    addressBook.print();

    cout << "\nSearching for  John  Doe..." <<
endl;
    Contact* contact = addressBook.search("John
Doe");
    if (contact != nullptr) {
        cout << "Found: " << contact->name << ",
" << contact->phoneNumber << endl;
    } else {
        cout << "Contact not found." << endl;
    }

    cout << "\nRemoving Jane Smith..." << endl;
    addressBook.remove("Jane Smith");

    cout << "\nUpdated Address Book:" << endl;
    addressBook.print();
```

```
    return 0;
}
```

Explanation:

- The `AddressBook` class stores contacts in a **binary search tree (BST)**, where contacts are inserted in lexicographical order based on the **name**.
- **Insertion**: A new contact is added using the `insert` method, which inserts the contact in the correct position in the tree.
- **Search**: The `search` method finds a contact by name efficiently.
- **Deletion**: The `remove` method removes a contact by name, ensuring the BST properties are maintained.

This example demonstrates how a BST can be used to implement an **address book**, where contacts can be stored, searched, and deleted efficiently based on the contact's name.

Conclusion

In this chapter, we covered **Binary Search Trees (BST)**, including their properties, insertion, deletion, and search operations. We explored a **real-world application** of BSTs by implementing an **address book**, where contacts are efficiently managed using BSTs. By understanding how BSTs work, you can apply this data structure to problems that require efficient search and sorting operations.

CHAPTER 13

AVL TREES – BALANCING BINARY SEARCH TREES

In this chapter, we will explore **AVL trees**, a type of **self-balancing binary search tree (BST)**. AVL trees are designed to keep the tree balanced after every insertion and deletion operation, ensuring that the tree remains efficient for searching, insertion, and deletion operations. We will discuss the **concept of self-balancing trees**, how **rotations** are used to maintain balance in AVL trees, and a **real-world example**: implementing **efficient searching in databases**.

Introduction to Self-Balancing Trees

A **self-balancing binary search tree** is a type of binary tree that automatically maintains its balance (i.e., keeps the height of the tree within limits) during insertions and deletions. The main advantage of self-balancing trees is that they ensure the height of the tree remains logarithmic relative to the number of nodes, which helps maintain efficient search times.

- In a **regular binary search tree (BST)**, the height of the tree can become skewed if elements are inserted in a sorted order, resulting in a tree that behaves like a linked list. This leads to inefficient operations (O(n) time complexity for search, insert, and delete).

- In a **self-balancing tree** (such as an **AVL tree** or **Red-Black tree**), the tree automatically adjusts itself to maintain balance, ensuring that the operations remain efficient (O(log n) time complexity).

AVL Tree is one of the oldest and most well-known self-balancing binary search trees. It ensures that for any node in the tree, the heights of its left and right subtrees differ by no more than **one**. This constraint ensures that the tree remains balanced and operations are efficient.

Rotations for Balancing AVL Trees

An important aspect of maintaining balance in an AVL tree is **rotations**. When the balance factor (the difference in height between the left and right subtrees) of a node becomes greater than 1 or less than -1, the tree is said to be **unbalanced**, and we need to perform rotations to restore balance.

There are four types of rotations used in AVL trees:

1. **Right Rotation (Single Rotation)**: This rotation is performed when the left subtree of a node is higher than the right subtree (left-heavy unbalanced node).

Example: If a node's left child has a left-heavy subtree, we perform a **right rotation** to balance the tree.

Right Rotation Process:

- The left child of the unbalanced node becomes the new root.
- The unbalanced node becomes the right child of the new root.

Illustration:

```markdown
    30
   /
  20
 /
```

10 (Right rotation around 30)

```
  20
 / \
10   30
vbnet
```

2. **Left Rotation (Single Rotation)**:

This rotation is performed when the right subtree of a node is higher than the left subtree (right-heavy unbalanced node).

Example: If a node's right child has a right-heavy subtree, we perform a **left rotation** to balance the tree.

Left Rotation Process:
- The right child of the unbalanced node becomes the new root.
- The unbalanced node becomes the left child of the new root.

Illustration:
markdown

```
    10
      \
       20
         \
          30
```

(Left rotation around 10)

```
   20
  /  \
10    30
```
pgsql

3. **Left-Right Rotation (Double Rotation)**:
This rotation is required when the left subtree
of the unbalanced node is **right-heavy**.

Left-Right Rotation Process:
- First, perform a **left rotation** on the left
child.
- Then, perform a **right rotation** on the
unbalanced node.

Illustration:

```
    30
   /
10
   \
    20
```

(Left-right rotation around 30)

```
    20
   /  \
  10   30
pgsql
```

4. **Right-Left Rotation (Double Rotation)**:

143

This rotation is required when the right subtree of the unbalanced node is **left-heavy**.

Right-Left Rotation Process:
- First, perform a **right rotation** on the right child.
- Then, perform a **left rotation** on the unbalanced node.

Illustration:
markdown

```
    10
      \
        30
       /
    20
```

(Right-left rotation around 10)

```
    20
   /  \
  10    30
```
rust

Each of these rotations helps maintain the AVL property by ensuring that the heights of the left and right subtrees never differ by more than one, thereby keeping the tree balanced.

Implementing AVL Trees in C++

To implement an AVL tree in C++, we need to define a tree structure and incorporate balancing logic during insertion and deletion operations. Below is a basic implementation of the **insert** operation with rotations to maintain balance.

AVL Tree Implementation in C++:

```cpp
#include <iostream>
using namespace std;

struct Node {
 int data;
 Node* left;
 Node* right;
 int height;

 Node(int value) : data(value), left(nullptr),
right(nullptr), height(1) {}
};

class AVLTree {
private:
```

```cpp
Node* root;

// Utility function to get the height of a node
int height(Node* node) {
    return (node == nullptr) ? 0 : node->height;
}

// Utility function to get the balance factor of
a node
int getBalance(Node* node) {
    return (node == nullptr) ? 0 : height(node->left) - height(node->right);
}

// Right rotation
Node* rightRotate(Node* y) {
    Node* x = y->left;
    Node* T2 = x->right;

    // Perform rotation
    x->right = y;
    y->left = T2;

    // Update heights
    y->height = max(height(y->left), height(y->right)) + 1;
    x->height = max(height(x->left), height(x->right)) + 1;
```

```cpp
    // Return new root
    return x;
}


// Left rotation
Node* leftRotate(Node* x) {
    Node* y = x->right;
    Node* T2 = y->left;

    // Perform rotation
    y->left = x;
    x->right = T2;

    // Update heights
    x->height = max(height(x->left), height(x->right)) + 1;
    y->height = max(height(y->left), height(y->right)) + 1;

    // Return new root
    return y;
}


// Insert a node and balance the tree
Node* insert(Node* node, int value) {
    // Step 1: Perform normal BST insert
    if (node == nullptr) {
        return new Node(value);
    }
```

```cpp
    if (value < node->data) {
        node->left = insert(node->left, value);
    } else if (value > node->data) {
        node->right    =    insert(node->right,
value);
    } else {  // Duplicate values are not allowed
        return node;
    }

    // Step 2: Update height of this ancestor
node
    node->height    =    max(height(node->left),
height(node->right)) + 1;

    // Step 3: Get the balance factor
    int balance = getBalance(node);

    // Step 4: Perform rotations to balance the
tree
    // Left Left case
    if (balance > 1 && value < node->left->data)
{
        return rightRotate(node);
    }

    // Right Right case
    if (balance < -1 && value > node->right-
>data) {
```

```cpp
        return leftRotate(node);
    }


    // Left Right case
    if (balance > 1 && value > node->left->data)
{

        node->left = leftRotate(node->left);
        return rightRotate(node);
    }


    // Right Left case
    if (balance < -1 && value < node->right-
>data) {
        node->right = rightRotate(node->right);
        return leftRotate(node);
    }


    // Return the (unchanged) node pointer
    return node;
 }

public:
 AVLTree() : root(nullptr) {}

 void insert(int value) {
    root = insert(root, value);
 }

 void inOrder(Node* node) {
```

149

```cpp
    if (node != nullptr) {
        inOrder(node->left);
        cout << node->data << " ";
        inOrder(node->right);
    }
  }

  void printInOrder() {
      inOrder(root);
  }
};

int main() {
  AVLTree tree;
  tree.insert(30);
  tree.insert(20);
  tree.insert(40);
  tree.insert(10);
  tree.insert(5);
  tree.insert(3);

  cout << "In-order traversal of the AVL tree: ";
  tree.printInOrder();   // Output: 3 5 10 20 30 40

  return 0;
}
```

Explanation:

- The `Node` structure represents each node in the AVL tree, with data, left and right child pointers, and the height of the node.
- The `AVLTree` class includes functions for:
  - **Rotations**: `leftRotate` and `rightRotate` perform the necessary rotations to restore balance.
  - **Insertion**: The `insert` function adds a node and then checks if the tree is unbalanced, performing rotations as necessary.
  - **Traversal**: The `inOrder` function performs an **in-order traversal** of the tree, printing nodes in sorted order.

Real-World Example: Implementing Efficient Searching in Databases

AVL trees are widely used in **databases** for indexing purposes because of their efficient search, insertion, and deletion operations. In a database, an **index** is used to quickly retrieve records based on search criteria. An AVL tree provides a balanced structure that allows for quick lookups, even as the database grows in size.

In a database indexing system, records are stored in an AVL tree where each node contains a unique key (such as a record ID) and a pointer to the record. The AVL tree ensures that the index remains balanced, which means search operations (like finding a record by key) are always efficient, with time complexity of **O(log n)**.

Conclusion

In this chapter, we explored **AVL trees**, a type of self-balancing binary search tree. We discussed how AVL trees maintain balance through rotations, and we implemented the **insert** operation with balancing in C++. We also explored a **real-world application** of AVL trees in **database indexing**, where efficient searching, insertion, and deletion operations are essential. By understanding AVL trees and their balancing mechanisms, you can apply them to solve complex problems that require dynamic data structures with optimal performance.

CHAPTER 14

HEAPS – PRIORITY QUEUES AND APPLICATIONS

In this chapter, we will explore **heaps**, a specialized tree-based data structure used to efficiently implement **priority queues**. We will cover the two main types of heaps: **min-heaps** and **max-heaps**, and how they are implemented. Additionally, we will examine **real-world applications** of heaps, particularly in **task scheduling** and **job queuing** within operating systems.

Understanding Heap Structures (Min-Heaps, Max-Heaps)

A **heap** is a complete binary tree that satisfies the **heap property**. This property is different depending on the type of heap:

- **Min-Heap**: In a min-heap, the value of each node is **smaller** than or equal to the values of its children. The smallest element is always at the **root**.
- **Max-Heap**: In a max-heap, the value of each node is **larger** than or equal to the values of its children. The largest element is always at the **root**.

Both types of heaps allow for efficient retrieval of the minimum or maximum element, respectively, in constant time **O(1)**. Heaps are usually implemented using arrays for simplicity.

Heap Properties:

1. **Complete Binary Tree**: Heaps are complete binary trees, meaning all levels of the tree are fully filled except possibly the last level, which is filled from left to right.
2. **Heap Property**: In a min-heap, the value of each parent node is smaller than or equal to the values of its children. In a max-heap, the value of each parent node is larger than or equal to the values of its children.

Visual Examples:

1. **Min-Heap**:

```markdown

    10
   /  \
  20    30
  / \
40    50
```

   o   In a min-heap, 10 is the smallest element, and every parent is smaller than its children.
2. **Max-Heap**:

markdown

```
    50
   /  \
  30   20
 /  \
10   5
```

- o In a max-heap, 50 is the largest element, and every parent is larger than its children.

Implementing Heaps for Priority Queues

A **priority queue** is an abstract data structure that allows us to insert elements and efficiently extract the element with the highest (or lowest) priority. Heaps are ideal for implementing priority queues because they allow insertion and extraction of the root element in **O(log n)** time.

A **min-heap** can be used for a **priority queue** where the element with the **lowest value** (highest priority) is removed first. A **max-heap** can be used for a priority queue where the element with the **highest value** (highest priority) is removed first.

Operations in a Heap-Based Priority Queue:

- **Insert**: Insert a new element into the heap and restore the heap property.

155

- **Extract-Min/Max**: Remove and return the root element (min or max), and restore the heap property.
- **Peek**: Return the root element without removing it.

Implementing a Min-Heap for a Priority Queue in C++:

cpp

```cpp
#include <iostream>
#include <vector>
using namespace std;

class MinHeap {
private:
    vector<int> heap;

    // Helper function to heapify the tree at a
given index
    void heapify(int index) {
        int left = 2 * index + 1;
        int right = 2 * index + 2;
        int smallest = index;

        if (left < heap.size() && heap[left] <
heap[smallest]) {
            smallest = left;
        }
        if (right < heap.size() && heap[right] <
heap[smallest]) {
```

```
            smallest = right;
        }


        if (smallest != index) {
            swap(heap[index], heap[smallest]);
            heapify(smallest);    // Recursively
heapify the affected subtree
        }
    }


    // Helper function to insert an element into
the heap
    void insertHeap(int value) {
        heap.push_back(value);      // Add   the
element at the end of the vector
        int index = heap.size() - 1;


        // Reorder the heap by bubbling up the
new element
        while (index > 0 && heap[(index - 1) / 2]
> heap[index]) {
            swap(heap[(index   -   1)   /   2],
heap[index]);
            index = (index - 1) / 2;
        }
    }


public:
```

```cpp
    // Function to insert a new value into the
priority queue (min-heap)
    void insert(int value) {
        insertHeap(value);
    }

    // Function to extract the element with the
minimum value (root)
    int extractMin() {
        if (heap.empty()) {
            cout << "Heap is empty!" << endl;
            return -1;
        }

        int minValue = heap[0];  // The root of
the heap is the minimum
        heap[0] = heap.back();  // Move the last
element to the root
        heap.pop_back();    // Remove  the  last
element

        heapify(0);  // Restore the heap property
by heapifying from the root
        return minValue;
    }

    // Function to return the minimum element
(root)
    int peek() {
```

```cpp
        if (heap.empty()) {
            cout << "Heap is empty!" << endl;
            return -1;
        }
        return heap[0];
    }

    // Function to check if the heap is empty
    bool isEmpty() {
        return heap.empty();
    }

    // Function to print the contents of the heap
    void print() {
        for (int value : heap) {
            cout << value << " ";
        }
        cout << endl;
    }
};

int main() {
    MinHeap pq;

    pq.insert(10);
    pq.insert(20);
    pq.insert(5);
    pq.insert(30);
    pq.insert(15);
```

```
    cout << "Priority Queue (Min-Heap): ";
    pq.print();

    cout << "Extract Min: " << pq.extractMin() <<
endl;
    pq.print();

    cout << "Peek: " << pq.peek() << endl;
    return 0;
}
```

Explanation:

- The `MinHeap` class implements a priority queue where the minimum value is always at the root of the heap.
- The `heapify` function restores the heap property after a removal or insertion.
- The `insert` function adds an element to the heap, maintaining the heap property by bubbling the element up.
- The `extractMin` function removes the root element (the minimum value) and restores the heap property by bubbling the new root down.
- The `peek` function allows us to view the minimum element without removing it.
- The `print` function displays the current elements in the heap.

160

Real-World Example: Task Scheduling and Job Queuing in Operating Systems

One of the most important applications of **heaps** is in **task scheduling** within operating systems. Operating systems often need to manage processes that need to be executed, and these processes can have different **priorities**.

A **priority queue** implemented using a heap can be used to schedule tasks. The operating system can assign priorities to tasks, and the heap will always allow the scheduler to quickly retrieve the highest-priority task for execution.

Example:

- Each task is represented by a structure that contains the task's **priority** and **task details**.
- Tasks with higher priority are placed at the root of the heap.
- The operating system **extracts** the task with the highest priority from the heap (the root) for execution.

For example, consider the following **task scheduling** in an operating system using a **max-heap**:

1. Tasks are inserted into the heap with a priority value.

2. When the CPU is ready to process a task, the scheduler **extracts the highest-priority task** (the root of the heap).

3. The scheduler executes the task, and once it completes, the next highest-priority task is processed.

Task Scheduler Example:

cpp

```cpp
#include <iostream>
#include <vector>
#include <string>
using namespace std;

struct Task {
    string name;
    int priority;

    Task(string n, int p) : name(n), priority(p)
{}
};

class TaskScheduler {
private:
    vector<Task> heap;

    void heapify(int index) {
        int left = 2 * index + 1;
        int right = 2 * index + 2;
```

```cpp
        int highest = index;

        if    (left    <    heap.size()    &&
heap[left].priority > heap[highest].priority) {
            highest = left;
        }
        if    (right    <    heap.size()    &&
heap[right].priority > heap[highest].priority) {
            highest = right;
        }

        if (highest != index) {
            swap(heap[index], heap[highest]);
            heapify(highest);
        }
    }

    void insertHeap(Task task) {
        heap.push_back(task);
        int index = heap.size() - 1;

        while (index > 0 && heap[(index - 1) /
2].priority < heap[index].priority) {
            swap(heap[(index   -   1)   /   2],
heap[index]);
            index = (index - 1) / 2;
        }
    }
```

```cpp
public:
    void insertTask(string name, int priority) {
        Task newTask(name, priority);
        insertHeap(newTask);
    }

    void processTask() {
        if (heap.empty()) {
            cout << "No tasks to process!" <<
endl;
            return;
        }

        Task highestPriorityTask = heap[0];
        cout << "Processing Task: " <<
highestPriorityTask.name << " with priority " <<
highestPriorityTask.priority << endl;

        // Remove the highest priority task and
restore the heap property
        heap[0] = heap.back();
        heap.pop_back();
        heapify(0);
    }

    bool isEmpty() {
        return heap.empty();
    }
};
```

164

```
int main() {
    TaskScheduler scheduler;

    scheduler.insertTask("Task 1", 5);
    scheduler.insertTask("Task 2", 3);
    scheduler.insertTask("Task 3", 8);
    scheduler.insertTask("Task 4", 6);

    while (!scheduler.isEmpty()) {
        scheduler.processTask();
    }

    return 0;
}
```

Explanation:

- The `TaskScheduler` class uses a **max-heap** to store tasks. Each task has a `name` and a `priority`.
- The `insertTask` method adds a new task to the heap, and the `processTask` method removes and processes the highest-priority task.
- The `heapify` function ensures that after removing a task, the heap property is maintained.

Conclusion

In this chapter, we explored **heaps**, a highly efficient data structure used to implement **priority queues**. We discussed **min-heaps** and **max-heaps**, focusing on their ability to retrieve the minimum or maximum element in constant time. We also implemented a **priority queue** using a min-heap in C++ and examined a **real-world application** of heaps in **task scheduling** within operating systems, where tasks are managed and executed based on priority. Heaps are an essential tool for efficient resource management in many real-world systems.

CHAPTER 15

GRAPHS – REPRESENTATION AND ALGORITHMS

In this chapter, we will delve into **graphs**, one of the most versatile data structures in computer science. Graphs are used to represent networks of relationships, such as **social networks**, **recommendation systems**, and **communication networks**. We will explore different types of graphs, including **directed**, **undirected**, **weighted**, and **unweighted** graphs, and discuss the two most common ways of representing graphs: **adjacency matrix** and **adjacency list**. Additionally, we will examine a **real-world example** of graphs in **social networks and recommendation systems**.

Introduction to Graphs (Directed, Undirected, Weighted, Unweighted)

A **graph** is a collection of **vertices** (also called **nodes**) connected by **edges** (also called **arcs**). Graphs are a powerful tool for modeling complex relationships in various fields, such as computer science, social sciences, transportation, and biology.

Graphs can be classified into the following types:

1. **Directed Graphs (DiGraphs)**:
   - In a **directed graph**, each edge has a **direction**, meaning it goes from one vertex to another (from **source** to **destination**).
   - **Example**: A **web page** pointing to another web page (directed edge from one URL to another).
   - **Notation**: The edge is represented as **(u, v)**, where **u** is the starting vertex and **v** is the ending vertex.

2. **Undirected Graphs**:
   - In an **undirected graph**, edges have **no direction**. The relationship between the vertices is bidirectional.
   - **Example**: A **friendship** in a social network, where both users are connected equally.
   - **Notation**: The edge is represented as **{u, v}**, where there is no direction.

3. **Weighted Graphs**:
   - A **weighted graph** assigns a **weight** (or cost) to each edge, representing the **cost, distance**, or **time** between the connected vertices.
   - **Example**: A **road network**, where the weight of the edge could represent the distance between two cities.

- o **Notation**: The edge is represented as **(u, v, w)**, where **w** is the weight of the edge between vertices **u** and **v**.

4. **Unweighted Graphs**:

   - o An **unweighted graph** has edges with no associated weights, meaning all edges are treated equally.

   - o **Example**: A **friendship network** where connections between people are either present or absent, with no specific "cost" attached.

   - o **Notation**: The edge is represented as **(u, v)**, with no additional data.

Adjacency Matrix and Adjacency List Representations

Graphs can be represented in several ways, but two of the most common methods are the **adjacency matrix** and the **adjacency list**.

1. **Adjacency Matrix**:

   - o An **adjacency matrix** is a 2D array used to represent a graph. The matrix is of size **V × V**, where **V** is the number of vertices in the graph. Each entry in the matrix indicates whether an edge exists between two vertices.

o For a **directed graph**, the entry `matrix[u][v]` = `1` indicates there is an edge from vertex **u** to vertex **v**. For an **undirected graph**, `matrix[u][v]` = `matrix[v][u]` = `1` indicates that the edge is bidirectional.

o In a **weighted graph**, the entry `matrix[u][v]` contains the weight of the edge, or `0` if no edge exists.

Example of an adjacency matrix for an undirected graph:

css

```
    A  B  C  D
A   0  1  1  0
B   1  0  1  1
C   1  1  0  1
D   0  1  1  0
```

o This matrix represents the following graph:

- A is connected to B and C.
- B is connected to A, C, and D.
- C is connected to A, B, and D.
- D is connected to B and C.

Pros of Adjacency Matrix:

- o Fast lookups for whether an edge exists between two vertices (**O(1)** time complexity).
- o Simple representation of graphs, especially useful for dense graphs (many edges).

Cons of Adjacency Matrix:

- o Takes **O(V^2)** space, which can be inefficient for sparse graphs (graphs with few edges).
- o Inserting or deleting edges requires modifying the matrix, which can be slow.

2. **Adjacency List**:
   - o An **adjacency list** represents a graph as an array of lists (or a hash map of lists), where each list corresponds to a vertex and contains all the adjacent vertices (neighbors).
   - o For an **undirected graph**, each edge is represented twice: once in the adjacency list of each of the two connected vertices.
   - o In a **weighted graph**, each list contains pairs of adjacent vertices and the corresponding edge weight.

Example of an adjacency list for the same graph:

```mathematica
A: [B, C]
```

```
B: [A, C, D]
C: [A, B, D]
D: [B, C]
```

Pros of Adjacency List:

- o Space-efficient, using only **O(E + V)** space, where **E** is the number of edges and **V** is the number of vertices. This is much more efficient for sparse graphs.
- o Efficient for iterating over all neighbors of a vertex (**O(degree(u))** time complexity).

Cons of Adjacency List:

- o Slightly slower for checking if an edge exists between two vertices (requires iterating over the list of neighbors).
- o Not as efficient for dense graphs, as it requires more memory for each vertex.

Real-World Example: Social Networks and Recommendation Systems

Graphs are commonly used in **social networks** and **recommendation systems** to model relationships and make personalized suggestions.

1. **Social Networks**: In a social network, users are represented as **vertices**, and their **relationships** (e.g., friendships, followers) are represented as **edges**. A user can have multiple friends (neighbors), and the graph structure allows us to easily find connections between users.

   Example:

   - A **directed graph** could be used to represent **followers** in a social media platform like Twitter, where an edge from **User A** to **User B** indicates that **A follows B**.
   - An **undirected graph** could be used to represent **friendships** in a platform like Facebook, where an edge between **User A** and **User B** means they are both friends.

2. **Recommendation Systems**: In **recommendation systems**, graphs are used to suggest items (such as movies, products, or songs) based on a user's preferences. The graph can represent users as vertices and the items they have interacted with (rated, bought, watched, etc.) as edges.

   For example:

o A **user-item graph** can be used where **users** are connected to **items** they have rated or interacted with.

o A **collaborative filtering** algorithm can be applied to recommend items to users based on the preferences of similar users (neighbors in the graph).

Example of a recommendation graph:

o **Users** and **Movies** are nodes in the graph.

o An edge between **User A** and **Movie X** indicates that User A has rated Movie X.

Conclusion

In this chapter, we covered **graphs**, a powerful and flexible data structure for modeling complex relationships. We discussed the key types of graphs: **directed**, **undirected**, **weighted**, and **unweighted**, and explored two common ways to represent graphs: the **adjacency matrix** and the **adjacency list**. Additionally, we examined **real-world applications** of graphs in **social networks** and **recommendation systems**, demonstrating their utility in modeling relationships and making predictions. By understanding graphs and their representations, you are now equipped to apply this data structure to solve problems in a wide variety of domains.

CHAPTER 16

DEPTH-FIRST SEARCH (DFS) AND BREADTH-FIRST SEARCH (BFS)

In this chapter, we will explore two fundamental algorithms for traversing or searching graphs: **Depth-First Search (DFS)** and **Breadth-First Search (BFS)**. These algorithms are widely used in various applications such as **maze solving**, **network routing**, and **graph traversal**. We will explain both algorithms, discuss their working principles, and look at real-world use cases where these algorithms are applied.

Explanation of DFS and BFS Algorithms

1. Depth-First Search (DFS):

DFS is an algorithm used to traverse or search a graph or tree. The idea behind DFS is to explore as far as possible along a branch before backtracking. This means that DFS explores a node's children before exploring the siblings of the node.

Steps of DFS:

175

1. Start at the root node (or any arbitrary node in the graph).

2. Visit the node.

3. Visit all unvisited children of the node (explore deeper).

4. Backtrack to the previous node once all children have been visited.

5. Repeat the process until all nodes have been visited.

DFS can be implemented using either **recursion** (using the call stack) or **explicit stack**.

DFS Example (Recursive): Given the following graph:

mathematica

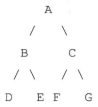

```
        A
      /   \
     B     C
    / \   / \
   D   E F   G
```

The DFS traversal would visit the nodes in this order: **A → B → D → E → C → F → G**.

C++ Code for DFS (recursive implementation):

cpp

```cpp
#include <iostream>
#include <vector>
```

```cpp
#include <stack>
using namespace std;

class Graph {
private:
    vector<vector<int>> adjList;
public:
    Graph(int vertices) {
        adjList.resize(vertices);
    }

    void addEdge(int u, int v) {
        adjList[u].push_back(v);
    }

    void DFS(int start, vector<bool>& visited) {
        visited[start] = true;
        cout << start << " ";

        // Visit all the unvisited adjacent nodes
        for (int neighbor : adjList[start]) {
            if (!visited[neighbor]) {
                DFS(neighbor, visited);
            }
        }
    }

    void dfsTraversal(int start) {
```

177

```cpp
        vector<bool>       visited(adjList.size(),
false);
        DFS(start, visited);
    }
};

int main() {
    Graph g(7);  // Create a graph with 7 nodes

    // Add edges to the graph
    g.addEdge(0, 1); // A -> B
    g.addEdge(0, 2); // A -> C
    g.addEdge(1, 3); // B -> D
    g.addEdge(1, 4); // B -> E
    g.addEdge(2, 5); // C -> F
    g.addEdge(2, 6); // C -> G

    cout << "DFS Traversal starting from node A
(0): ";
    g.dfsTraversal(0);  // Output: A B D E C F G
    return 0;
}
```

Explanation:

- In this implementation, the `DFS` function explores each node recursively, marking it as visited and exploring its adjacent nodes.

- The `dfsTraversal` function initializes the visited array and calls the DFS method starting from a given node.

2. Breadth-First Search (BFS):

BFS is an algorithm for traversing or searching a graph level by level, i.e., it visits all nodes at the present depth level before moving on to nodes at the next depth level. BFS explores a graph in a **breadth-first** manner, meaning it visits all nodes that are at a distance 1 from the source node, then all nodes at distance 2, and so on.

Steps of BFS:

1. Start at the root node (or any arbitrary node in the graph).
2. Visit the node and enqueue it.
3. While the queue is not empty:
   - Dequeue a node from the front of the queue.
   - Visit all unvisited adjacent nodes and enqueue them.
4. Repeat the process until all nodes have been visited.

BFS is often implemented using a **queue** to ensure nodes are processed level by level.

BFS Example: Given the following graph:

```
mathematica
```

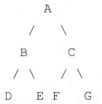

```
       A
      / \
     B   C
    / \ / \
   D  E F  G
```

The BFS traversal would visit the nodes in this order: **A → B → C → D → E → F → G**.

C++ Code for BFS (using a queue):

cpp

```cpp
#include <iostream>
#include <vector>
#include <queue>
using namespace std;

class Graph {
private:
    vector<vector<int>> adjList;
public:
    Graph(int vertices) {
        adjList.resize(vertices);
    }

    void addEdge(int u, int v) {
        adjList[u].push_back(v);
    }
```

```cpp
    void BFS(int start) {
        vector<bool>     visited(adjList.size(),
false);
        queue<int> q;

        visited[start] = true;
        q.push(start);

        while (!q.empty()) {
            int node = q.front();
            q.pop();
            cout << node << " ";

            for (int neighbor : adjList[node]) {
                if (!visited[neighbor]) {
                    visited[neighbor] = true;
                    q.push(neighbor);
                }
            }
        }
    }
};

int main() {
    Graph g(7);  // Create a graph with 7 nodes

    // Add edges to the graph
    g.addEdge(0, 1); // A -> B
```

```
g.addEdge(0, 2); // A -> C
g.addEdge(1, 3); // B -> D
g.addEdge(1, 4); // B -> E
g.addEdge(2, 5); // C -> F
g.addEdge(2, 6); // C -> G

cout << "BFS Traversal starting from node A
(0): ";
g.BFS(0);  // Output: A B C D E F G
return 0;
}
```

Explanation:

- In this implementation, the BFS function uses a queue to visit each node level by level.
- The BFS algorithm enqueues a node, processes it, and then enqueues all unvisited neighbors of the node.

Use Cases: Solving Mazes, Network Routing, and Graph Traversal

1. **Solving Mazes:**
   - **DFS** can be used to explore a maze by backtracking when a dead-end is reached, allowing us to find a path through the maze.
   - **BFS**, on the other hand, is often preferred for finding the **shortest path** in a maze, as it explores

all possible paths level by level, ensuring the first time it reaches the exit, it's the shortest path.

2. **Network Routing**:
   - o **BFS** is widely used in **network routing** to find the shortest path in terms of hops between nodes. For example, **routers** in a network can use BFS to find the shortest route to forward data packets to their destination.
   - o **DFS** might be used in network analysis, for example, to explore all possible routes between two nodes or to check for connectivity in a network.

3. **Graph Traversal**:
   - o **DFS** is useful for exploring all possible paths in a graph, detecting cycles, and solving problems like topological sorting (in **directed acyclic graphs**).
   - o **BFS** is commonly used for finding the **shortest path** in **unweighted graphs** or for level-order traversal (e.g., in trees).

Conclusion

In this chapter, we explored **Depth-First Search (DFS)** and **Breadth-First Search (BFS)**, two fundamental graph traversal algorithms. DFS explores a graph deeply before backtracking, while BFS explores a graph level by level. Both algorithms are widely used in various applications, including **solving mazes**, **network routing**, and general **graph traversal**. Understanding these algorithms and their real-world applications is key to solving complex problems in computer science and engineering. With the provided C++ code examples, you now have the tools to implement these algorithms in your own projects.

CHAPTER 17

SHORTEST PATH ALGORITHMS – DIJKSTRA'S AND BELLMAN-FORD

In this chapter, we will explore **shortest path algorithms**, focusing on two widely used algorithms: **Dijkstra's algorithm** and the **Bellman-Ford algorithm**. These algorithms are essential for finding the shortest path between nodes in a graph, which is a critical operation in various applications such as **GPS navigation systems**. We will discuss the theory behind each algorithm, how to implement them, and provide a **real-world application** in GPS navigation systems.

Introduction to Shortest Path Algorithms

Finding the shortest path in a graph is a common problem in computer science, especially in applications involving **transportation networks, communication networks**, and **route planning**. The objective is to find the **minimum cost** (or distance) from a **source node** to a **destination node** in a weighted graph, where the edges represent the cost of traveling from one node to another.

There are two common types of graphs:

- **Weighted Graphs**: Where each edge has an associated weight (e.g., distance, time, cost).
- **Unweighted Graphs**: Where all edges are treated as having the same weight (can be handled by simpler algorithms like BFS).

The two main algorithms we'll focus on are:

1. **Dijkstra's Algorithm**: An efficient algorithm for finding the shortest path in a graph with **non-negative edge weights**.
2. **Bellman-Ford Algorithm**: A more general algorithm that works with graphs that may have **negative edge weights**, but is less efficient than Dijkstra's.

Dijkstra's Algorithm

Dijkstra's algorithm is a **greedy algorithm** used to find the shortest path from a source node to all other nodes in a graph with **non-negative edge weights**. The algorithm maintains a set of **visited nodes** and iteratively expands the shortest path from the source node to other nodes.

Steps of Dijkstra's Algorithm:

1. Initialize the distance to the source node as 0 and the distance to all other nodes as infinity.

2. Set the source node as the current node and mark it as visited.

3. For each unvisited neighbor of the current node, calculate the tentative distance through the current node.

4. After visiting all neighbors, choose the unvisited node with the smallest tentative distance and set it as the current node.

5. Repeat steps 3 and 4 until all nodes are visited or the smallest tentative distance is infinity (meaning unreachable nodes).

Example of Dijkstra's Algorithm: Given the following weighted graph:

css

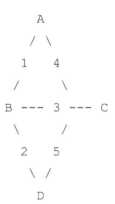

Dijkstra's Algorithm will find the shortest path from node **A** to all other nodes in the graph.

C++ Code for Dijkstra's Algorithm:

cpp

```cpp
#include <iostream>
#include <vector>
#include <climits>
#include <set>
using namespace std;

class Graph {
private:
    int V;
    vector<vector<pair<int, int>>> adj;

public:
    Graph(int V) {
        this->V = V;
        adj.resize(V);
    }

    void addEdge(int u, int v, int weight) {
        adj[u].push_back({v, weight});
        adj[v].push_back({u,  weight});  // For undirected graph
    }
```

```cpp
void dijkstra(int start) {
    vector<int>  dist(V,   INT_MAX);      //
Initialize all distances to infinity
    dist[start] = 0;   // Distance to the
source is 0

    set<pair<int, int>> pq;   // Priority
queue to pick the node with the smallest distance
    pq.insert({0, start});    // Insert the
source node with distance 0

    while (!pq.empty()) {
        int u = pq.begin()->second;   // Get
the node with the smallest distance
        pq.erase(pq.begin());

        // Explore the neighbors of u
        for (auto neighbor : adj[u]) {
            int v = neighbor.first;
            int weight = neighbor.second;

            // If a shorter path to v is
found
            if (dist[u] + weight < dist[v])
{
                // Remove the old pair and
insert the new one with updated distance
                if (dist[v] != INT_MAX) {
```

189

```cpp
pq.erase(pq.find({dist[v], v}));
                        }
                        dist[v] = dist[u] + weight;
                        pq.insert({dist[v], v});
                    }
                }
            }


        // Print the shortest distances
        for (int i = 0; i < V; i++) {
            cout << "Distance from " << start <<
" to " << i << " is " << dist[i] << endl;
        }
    }
};

int main() {
    Graph g(4);
    g.addEdge(0, 1, 1);   // A-B with weight 1
    g.addEdge(0, 2, 4);   // A-C with weight 4
    g.addEdge(1, 2, 3);   // B-C with weight 3
    g.addEdge(1, 3, 2);   // B-D with weight 2
    g.addEdge(2, 3, 5);   // C-D with weight 5

    g.dijkstra(0);   // Run Dijkstra's algorithm
starting from node A (0)

    return 0;
```

}

Explanation:

- The graph is represented using an adjacency list `adj`, where each node stores its neighbors and the weights of the edges.
- The `dijkstra` function uses a **set** (priority queue) to always select the node with the smallest tentative distance.
- The algorithm iterates over the neighbors of the current node, updating the shortest distances to each neighbor.

Bellman-Ford Algorithm

The **Bellman-Ford algorithm** is another algorithm for finding the shortest paths in a graph. It is capable of handling graphs with **negative edge weights** but is less efficient than Dijkstra's algorithm. Bellman-Ford can also detect **negative weight cycles** in the graph, which is something Dijkstra's algorithm cannot do.

Steps of Bellman-Ford Algorithm:

1. Initialize the distance to the source node as 0 and the distance to all other nodes as infinity.
2. For each edge, if the distance to the destination node can be shortened by taking the edge, update the distance.

3. Repeat the above step **V-1 times**, where **V** is the number of vertices.

4. Check for negative weight cycles by performing one more iteration. If any distance can still be updated, a negative weight cycle exists.

C++ Code for Bellman-Ford Algorithm:

cpp

```cpp
#include <iostream>
#include <vector>
#include <climits>
using namespace std;

class Graph {
private:
    int V;
    vector<vector<pair<int, int>>> adj;

public:
    Graph(int V) {
        this->V = V;
        adj.resize(V);
    }

    void addEdge(int u, int v, int weight) {
        adj[u].push_back({v, weight});
    }
```

```cpp
void bellmanFord(int start) {
    vector<int>  dist(V,  INT_MAX);       //
Initialize all distances to infinity
    dist[start] = 0;   // Distance to the
source is 0

    // Relax edges repeatedly
    for (int i = 1; i < V; i++) {
        for (int u = 0; u < V; u++) {
            for (auto neighbor : adj[u]) {
                int v = neighbor.first;
                int       weight       =
neighbor.second;
                if (dist[u] != INT_MAX &&
dist[u] + weight < dist[v]) {
                    dist[v]  =  dist[u]  +
weight;
                }
            }
        }
    }

    // Check for negative-weight cycles
    for (int u = 0; u < V; u++) {
        for (auto neighbor : adj[u]) {
            int v = neighbor.first;
            int weight = neighbor.second;
```

```cpp
                if (dist[u] != INT_MAX && dist[u]
+ weight < dist[v]) {
                    cout    <<    "Graph    contains
negative weight cycle" << endl;
                    return;
                }
            }
        }

        // Print the shortest distances
        for (int i = 0; i < V; i++) {
            cout << "Distance from " << start <<
" to " << i << " is " << dist[i] << endl;
        }
    }
};

int main() {
    Graph g(5);
    g.addEdge(0, 1, -1);   // A -> B with weight
-1
    g.addEdge(0, 2, 4);    // A -> C with weight
4
    g.addEdge(1, 2, 3);    // B -> C with weight
3
    g.addEdge(1, 3, 2);    // B -> D with weight
2
    g.addEdge(1, 4, 2);    // B -> E with weight
2
```

```
    g.addEdge(3, 2, 5);    // D -> C with weight
5

    g.addEdge(3, 1, 1);    // D -> B with weight
1

    g.addEdge(4, 3, -3);   // E -> D with weight
-3

    g.bellmanFord(0);      //  Run  Bellman-Ford
starting from node A (0)

    return 0;
}
```

Explanation:

- The `bellmanFord` function iterates **V-1 times** over all edges to update the shortest distances.
- The second loop checks for negative weight cycles by trying to update distances once more after **V-1 iterations**.

Real-World Example: GPS Navigation Systems

A **GPS navigation system** uses **shortest path algorithms** to calculate the most efficient route from a starting point to a destination. This involves modeling roads and intersections as a **graph**, where:

- **Nodes** represent locations (e.g., cities or intersections).

195

- **Edges** represent roads connecting these locations, with weights representing the **distance**, **time**, or **cost** of traveling along the road.
- **Dijkstra's Algorithm** is commonly used in GPS systems when all roads have non-negative weights, as it efficiently computes the shortest path between the current location and the destination.
- **Bellman-Ford** might be used when road weights can be negative (e.g., tolls or negative travel time adjustments) or for detecting negative cycles in transportation networks (though it's less efficient for this use case).

Example:

- A **driver** uses a GPS system that computes the fastest route based on real-time traffic data. The GPS system may use **Dijkstra's algorithm** to find the shortest travel time by considering distances and road conditions as weights on edges.

Conclusion

In this chapter, we explored **shortest path algorithms**, focusing on **Dijkstra's algorithm** and the **Bellman-Ford algorithm**. We discussed how Dijkstra's algorithm is efficient for graphs with non-negative edge weights, while Bellman-Ford is more general and can handle negative edge weights. We also examined **real-world applications** of these algorithms, particularly in **GPS navigation systems**, where they are used to find the fastest route between locations. By understanding these algorithms and their applications, you are now equipped to apply shortest path algorithms to a variety of problems in graph theory and real-world systems.

CHAPTER 18

DYNAMIC PROGRAMMING – OPTIMIZATION TECHNIQUES

In this chapter, we will explore **dynamic programming (DP)**, a powerful optimization technique used to solve complex problems by breaking them down into simpler subproblems. DP is particularly useful for problems where the solution can be constructed efficiently by reusing solutions to smaller subproblems. We will discuss the **concept of dynamic programming**, solve classic problems such as the **Fibonacci sequence** and the **knapsack problem**, and explore a **real-world use case**: optimizing **inventory management**.

Concept of Dynamic Programming (DP)

Dynamic programming is an algorithmic technique used for solving problems by dividing them into overlapping subproblems, solving each subproblem just once, and storing its solution in a table (usually a **2D array**, **array**, or **hash map**) to avoid redundant calculations. The core idea is to **reuse** solutions to smaller subproblems to build up the solution to the overall problem.

DP is generally used when the problem has the following characteristics:

- **Optimal Substructure**: The optimal solution to the problem can be constructed from the optimal solutions of its subproblems.
- **Overlapping Subproblems**: The problem can be broken down into subproblems that are solved multiple times.

There are two main approaches to implementing DP:

1. **Top-Down Approach (Memoization)**: This approach involves solving the problem recursively, storing solutions to subproblems as they are computed, and reusing them whenever the same subproblem is encountered.
2. **Bottom-Up Approach (Tabulation)**: This approach starts by solving the smallest subproblems first and builds up to the solution of the entire problem.

Solving Problems with Dynamic Programming

We will solve two classic problems using dynamic programming: the **Fibonacci sequence** and the **knapsack problem**.

1. Fibonacci Sequence Using DP

The **Fibonacci sequence** is a sequence of numbers in which each number is the sum of the two preceding ones, starting from 0 and 1. The Fibonacci sequence is commonly defined as:

r

```
F(0) = 0
F(1) = 1
F(n) = F(n-1) + F(n-2), for n > 1
```

Using DP, we can calculate the **n-th Fibonacci number** efficiently by storing previously computed Fibonacci numbers and reusing them.

C++ Code for Fibonacci Sequence Using DP (Memoization Approach):

cpp

```cpp
#include <iostream>
#include <vector>
using namespace std;

class Fibonacci {
private:
    vector<int> memo;
```

```cpp
public:
    Fibonacci(int n) {
        memo.resize(n + 1, -1);   // Initialize
memoization array
    }

    int fib(int n) {
        if (n <= 1) {
            return n;
        }
        if (memo[n] != -1) {
            return memo[n];  // Return the result
if already computed
        }
        memo[n] = fib(n - 1) + fib(n - 2);   //
Store the result in memo array
        return memo[n];
    }
};

int main() {
    int n = 10;
    Fibonacci fib(n);
    cout << "Fibonacci of " << n << " is " <<
fib.fib(n) << endl;  // Output: 55
    return 0;
}
```

Explanation:

- The `memo` array is used to store Fibonacci numbers that are computed to avoid redundant calculations.
- The `fib` function calculates Fibonacci numbers recursively, but it first checks if the result is already stored in the `memo` array. If it is, it simply returns the result from the array.

---

2. Knapsack Problem Using DP

The **0/1 knapsack problem** is a classic optimization problem where the goal is to select a subset of items that maximizes the total value without exceeding a weight limit. Given a set of items, each with a weight and a value, the problem is to find the maximum value of items that can be included in a knapsack of a fixed capacity.

Problem Definition:

- We are given **n** items, each with a value **v[i]** and a weight **w[i]**.
- We are given a knapsack with a weight capacity **W**.
- The objective is to maximize the total value of the selected items, without exceeding the weight capacity.

C++ Code for Solving the 0/1 Knapsack Problem Using DP (Tabulation Approach):

cpp

```cpp
#include <iostream>
#include <vector>
#include <algorithm>
using namespace std;

class Knapsack {
public:
    int knapSack(int W, const vector<int>& weights, const vector<int>& values, int n) {
        vector<vector<int>> dp(n + 1, vector<int>(W + 1, 0));  // DP table

        // Fill the DP table
        for (int i = 1; i <= n; i++) {
            for (int w = 1; w <= W; w++) {
                if (weights[i - 1] <= w) {
                    dp[i][w] = max(dp[i - 1][w],
dp[i - 1][w - weights[i - 1]] + values[i - 1]);
                } else {
                    dp[i][w] = dp[i - 1][w];
                }
            }
        }

        return dp[n][W];  // The maximum value in the knapsack
    }
```

```
};

int main() {
    int W = 50;   // Knapsack capacity
    vector<int> values = {60, 100, 120};  // Item
values
    vector<int> weights = {10, 20, 30};  // Item
weights
    int n = values.size();  // Number of items

    Knapsack knapsack;
    cout << "Maximum value in knapsack: " <<
knapsack.knapSack(W, weights, values, n) << endl;
// Output: 220
    return 0;
}
```

Explanation:

- The `dp` table stores the maximum value that can be obtained for each subproblem. Each cell `dp[i][w]` represents the maximum value that can be obtained with the first `i` items and a knapsack capacity of `w`.
- For each item, we check whether it can fit in the knapsack (i.e., if `weights[i-1] <= w`). If it can, we choose the maximum value between:
  - Not including the current item (`dp[i-1][w]`), and

204

- o Including the current item (`dp[i-1][w-weights[i-1]] + values[i-1]`).

The time complexity of this approach is **O(nW)**, where `n` is the number of items and `W` is the capacity of the knapsack.

Real-World Use Case: Optimizing Inventory Management

One real-world use of **dynamic programming** is in **inventory management**, where businesses aim to optimize the storage, ordering, and distribution of goods to minimize costs and maximize profits.

In an **inventory management system**, DP can be applied to problems like:

1. **Optimal stock levels**: Determining the best stock levels for various products to minimize storage costs while ensuring sufficient stock to meet demand.
2. **Order optimization**: Deciding on the best quantities to order from suppliers to minimize costs (taking into account bulk discounts, shipping fees, etc.).
3. **Resource allocation**: Allocating limited resources (e.g., warehouse space, employees) in a way that maximizes overall efficiency.

For example, consider a warehouse that stores multiple products, and the goal is to minimize the total cost of storing the products. The problem can be formulated as a **knapsack problem** where:

- The **items** are the products.
- The **weights** are the storage space required for each product.
- The **values** are the profits generated from storing and selling each product.

Using DP, you can calculate the optimal allocation of space in the warehouse to maximize profits while adhering to storage constraints.

Conclusion

In this chapter, we explored **dynamic programming (DP)**, an optimization technique that breaks down problems into smaller overlapping subproblems and solves them efficiently by storing the results. We solved two classic problems using DP: the **Fibonacci sequence** and the **0/1 knapsack problem**, demonstrating how DP can optimize solutions to complex problems. We also examined a **real-world application** of DP in **inventory management**, where DP can help businesses optimize stock levels and reduce costs. By mastering dynamic programming, you can solve a wide range of optimization problems more efficiently.

CHAPTER 19

GREEDY ALGORITHMS – MAKING OPTIMAL CHOICES

In this chapter, we will explore **greedy algorithms**, a class of algorithms that make a sequence of **locally optimal choices** in the hope that these choices lead to a globally optimal solution. Greedy algorithms are often used for **optimization problems**, where the goal is to find the best possible solution according to some criteria. We will discuss the principles behind greedy algorithms, solve classic problems such as **Huffman encoding** and **activity selection**, and explore a **real-world example** of **minimizing resource allocation in cloud computing**.

Understanding Greedy Algorithms

A **greedy algorithm** works by making a series of choices that are **locally optimal** at each step. These algorithms do not consider the global situation but instead focus on the immediate best option at each stage, hoping that these choices will lead to an optimal solution for the entire problem.

Key Characteristics of Greedy Algorithms:

1. **Greedy Choice Property**: A global optimal solution can be arrived at by selecting a local optimum at each step.

2. **Optimal Substructure**: A problem has an optimal substructure if an optimal solution to the problem can be constructed efficiently from optimal solutions of its subproblems.

While greedy algorithms are **simple** and often **efficient** (usually with time complexity of **O(n log n)** or better), they do not always produce the correct solution for every problem. Some problems require **backtracking** or **dynamic programming** to ensure that the optimal solution is found.

Solving Problems with Greedy Algorithms

We will now look at two classic examples where greedy algorithms are used effectively: **Huffman encoding** and **activity selection**.

1. Huffman Encoding

Huffman encoding is a popular algorithm used in **data compression**. It is used to represent characters with variable-length codes, with more frequent characters having shorter codes. The algorithm works by creating a **binary tree** where the most frequent characters are placed closer to the root, minimizing the total number of bits needed to represent the data.

Steps of Huffman Encoding:

1. Count the frequency of each character in the data.
2. Create a priority queue (min-heap) with nodes containing characters and their frequencies.
3. While there is more than one node in the queue:
   - Remove the two nodes with the lowest frequencies.
   - Create a new internal node with these two nodes as children and the sum of their frequencies as the frequency of the new node.
   - Insert the new node back into the queue.
4. The remaining node is the root of the Huffman tree.
5. Traverse the tree to assign binary codes to each character.

C++ Code for Huffman Encoding:

cpp

```
#include <iostream>
#include <queue>
#include <vector>
#include <unordered_map>
using namespace std;
```

```cpp
// A node in the Huffman tree
struct Node {
    char ch;
    int freq;
    Node* left;
    Node* right;

    Node(char character, int frequency) {
        ch = character;
        freq = frequency;
        left = right = nullptr;
    }
};


// Compare function for priority queue
struct Compare {
    bool operator()(Node* left, Node* right) {
        return left->freq > right->freq;  // Min-
heap based on frequency
    }
};


void printCodes(Node* root, string code) {
    if (root == nullptr) {
        return;
    }
    if (root->ch != '$') {
        cout << root->ch << ": " << code << endl;
    }
```

211

```cpp
    printCodes(root->left, code + "0");
    printCodes(root->right, code + "1");
}


void huffmanEncoding(string text) {
    unordered_map<char, int> freqMap;
    for (char ch : text) {
        freqMap[ch]++;
    }

    priority_queue<Node*,        vector<Node*>,
Compare> minHeap;

    // Create leaf nodes and add them to the
priority queue
    for (auto pair : freqMap) {
        minHeap.push(new        Node(pair.first,
pair.second));
    }

    // Build the Huffman tree
    while (minHeap.size() > 1) {
        Node* left = minHeap.top();
        minHeap.pop();
        Node* right = minHeap.top();
        minHeap.pop();

        Node* newNode = new Node('$', left->freq
+ right->freq);
```

```
        newNode->left = left;
        newNode->right = right;

        minHeap.push(newNode);
    }

    // Root of the Huffman tree
    Node* root = minHeap.top();
    printCodes(root, "");
}

int main() {
    string text = "this is an example for huffman
encoding";
    cout << "Huffman Codes for characters: \n";
    huffmanEncoding(text);
    return 0;
}
```

Explanation:

- The Node structure represents a character in the tree along with its frequency.

- We use a **priority queue (min-heap)** to always extract the two nodes with the lowest frequencies and combine them into a new internal node.

- The printCodes function recursively traverses the Huffman tree to generate the binary codes for each character.

213

- The algorithm builds the Huffman tree and outputs the **optimal binary encoding** for the characters.

---

2. Activity Selection Problem

The **activity selection problem** is a classic problem where we are given a set of activities with their start and finish times, and the goal is to select the maximum number of activities that do not overlap. The greedy approach to solving this problem is to always select the activity that finishes the earliest, allowing room for subsequent activities.

Steps of the Activity Selection Algorithm:

1. Sort the activities based on their finish times.
2. Select the first activity, and for each subsequent activity, select it if its start time is greater than or equal to the finish time of the previously selected activity.
3. Continue selecting activities until all activities are considered.

C++ Code for Activity Selection:

cpp

```cpp
#include <iostream>
#include <vector>
```

```cpp
#include <algorithm>
using namespace std;

struct Activity {
    int start, finish;
};

bool compare(Activity a, Activity b) {
    return a.finish < b.finish;    // Sort by
finish time
}

void          activitySelection(vector<Activity>&
activities) {
    sort(activities.begin(),    activities.end(),
compare);   // Sort activities by finish time

    int lastSelected = 0;
    cout << "Selected activities: \n";
    cout            <<           "("          <<
activities[lastSelected].start   <<    ",    "   <<
activities[lastSelected].finish << ")\n";

    for (int i = 1; i < activities.size(); i++)
{
        if          (activities[i].start          >=
activities[lastSelected].finish) {
            cout << "(" << activities[i].start <<
", " << activities[i].finish << ")\n";
```

```
                lastSelected = i;
            }
        }
    }

int main() {
    vector<Activity> activities = {{1, 3}, {2,
5}, {4, 6}, {7, 8}, {5, 7}, {8, 9}};
    activitySelection(activities);
    return 0;
}
```

Explanation:

- The `Activity` structure holds the start and finish times of an activity.
- The `compare` function is used to sort activities by their finish times in ascending order.
- The `activitySelection` function selects activities greedily by always picking the next activity that starts after the last selected activity finishes.

Real-World Example: Minimizing Resource Allocation in Cloud Computing

One practical application of **greedy algorithms** is in **cloud computing**, where resource allocation is a crucial task. The goal is to optimize the use of resources (e.g., CPU, memory, storage) while minimizing costs. Cloud service providers often need to allocate resources to different tasks or clients in a way that maximizes efficiency.

Problem: Suppose a cloud computing system needs to allocate **tasks** (e.g., data processing jobs) to **servers** in a way that minimizes the total time or cost. The problem can be formulated as an **activity selection problem** where:

- The **tasks** are activities.
- The **servers** are the available resources.
- The objective is to **minimize the total time** or **cost** by selecting tasks in an optimal sequence.

A **greedy approach** can be used to assign tasks to servers by selecting the tasks with the **shortest execution times** first, allowing the cloud system to complete as many tasks as possible within a given time frame. This method minimizes idle times and optimizes the use of resources.

Example:

- A cloud provider might use a **greedy scheduling algorithm** to assign tasks to the available servers in such a way that each server works on the shortest available task first, thus maximizing the number of tasks completed within a certain time limit.

217

Conclusion

In this chapter, we explored **greedy algorithms**, a class of algorithms that make **locally optimal choices** with the hope of finding a global optimum. We solved classic problems such as **Huffman encoding** for data compression and the **activity selection problem** for selecting non-overlapping activities. We also discussed a **real-world application** of greedy algorithms in **cloud computing**, where they are used to minimize resource allocation and optimize task scheduling. By understanding greedy algorithms, you can apply them to a wide range of optimization problems that require efficient solutions.

CHAPTER 20

DIVIDE AND CONQUER –
BREAKING PROBLEMS INTO
SUBPROBLEMS

In this chapter, we will explore **divide and conquer** algorithms, a powerful strategy for solving problems by breaking them into smaller subproblems, solving each subproblem recursively, and then combining the solutions to solve the overall problem. We will implement two classic divide and conquer algorithms: **Merge Sort** and **QuickSort**, and discuss their application in **sorting large datasets**, a real-world use case of this technique.

Introduction to Divide and Conquer Algorithms

Divide and conquer is an algorithmic paradigm that works by recursively breaking down a problem into smaller subproblems, solving the subproblems independently, and then combining their solutions to solve the original problem. This approach is particularly useful for problems that have the following characteristics:

219

1. **Subproblems**: The problem can be divided into smaller, similar subproblems.

2. **Independence**: The subproblems can be solved independently and do not rely on each other.

3. **Combine**: The solutions to the subproblems can be combined to form the solution to the original problem.

General Steps in Divide and Conquer:

1. **Divide**: Break the problem into smaller subproblems.

2. **Conquer**: Solve each subproblem recursively. If the subproblem is small enough, solve it directly.

3. **Combine**: Combine the solutions of the subproblems to form the solution to the original problem.

This paradigm is efficient for problems where the size of the problem can be reduced exponentially with each recursive step. It is often used in problems involving **sorting**, **searching**, **matrix operations**, and **graph algorithms**.

Implementing Algorithms: Merge Sort and QuickSort

Let's now look at two of the most famous **divide and conquer** algorithms: **Merge Sort** and **QuickSort**.

1. Merge Sort

Merge Sort is a classic **divide and conquer** algorithm that divides the input array into two halves, recursively sorts each half, and then merges the two sorted halves to produce the final sorted array.

Steps of Merge Sort:

1. **Divide**: Split the array into two halves.
2. **Conquer**: Recursively sort both halves.
3. **Combine**: Merge the two sorted halves into a single sorted array.

C++ Code for Merge Sort:

cpp

```cpp
#include <iostream>
#include <vector>
using namespace std;

// Function to merge two halves of the array
void merge(vector<int>& arr, int left, int mid,
int right) {
    int n1 = mid - left + 1;
    int n2 = right - mid;

    // Create temporary arrays
```

```cpp
    vector<int> leftArr(n1), rightArr(n2);


    //  data into temporary arrays
    for (int i = 0; i < n1; i++) {
        leftArr[i] = arr[left + i];
    }
    for (int i = 0; i < n2; i++) {
        rightArr[i] = arr[mid + 1 + i];
    }


    // Merge the temporary arrays back into the
original array
    int i = 0, j = 0, k = left;
    while (i < n1 && j < n2) {
        if (leftArr[i] <= rightArr[j]) {
            arr[k] = leftArr[i];
            i++;
        } else {
            arr[k] = rightArr[j];
            j++;
        }
        k++;
    }


    //  any remaining elements from leftArr
    while (i < n1) {
        arr[k] = leftArr[i];
        i++;
        k++;
```

```
    }

    //  any remaining elements from rightArr
    while (j < n2) {
        arr[k] = rightArr[j];
        j++;
        k++;
    }
}


// Merge sort function
void mergeSort(vector<int>& arr, int left, int
right) {
    if (left >= right) {
        return;
    }

    int mid = left + (right - left) / 2;

    // Recursively divide the array
    mergeSort(arr, left, mid);
    mergeSort(arr, mid + 1, right);

    // Merge the sorted halves
    merge(arr, left, mid, right);
}

int main() {
    vector<int> arr = {38, 27, 43, 3, 9, 82, 10};
```

```
cout << "Original array: ";
for (int num : arr) {
    cout << num << " ";
}
cout << endl;

mergeSort(arr, 0, arr.size() - 1);

cout << "Sorted array: ";
for (int num : arr) {
    cout << num << " ";
}
cout << endl;

return 0;
}
```

Explanation:

- The mergeSort function recursively divides the array into two halves, sorts them, and then merges them back together using the merge function.
- The time complexity of Merge Sort is **O(n log n)**, where n is the number of elements in the array, making it an efficient sorting algorithm.

2. QuickSort

QuickSort is another popular **divide and conquer** algorithm. It works by selecting a **pivot element** and partitioning the array into two subarrays: one with elements smaller than the pivot and one with elements larger than the pivot. The algorithm then recursively sorts the subarrays.

Steps of QuickSort:

1. **Choose a Pivot**: Select an element as the pivot (usually the first, last, or middle element).
2. **Partition**: Rearrange the array so that all elements less than the pivot are on its left and all elements greater than the pivot are on its right.
3. **Conquer**: Recursively apply the same process to the left and right subarrays.
4. **Combine**: The array is sorted once all the subarrays are sorted.

C++ Code for QuickSort:

cpp

```
#include <iostream>
#include <vector>
using namespace std;
```

```cpp
// Function to partition the array around a pivot
int partition(vector<int>& arr, int low, int
high) {
    int pivot = arr[high];   // Choose the last
element as the pivot
    int i = low - 1;   // Pointer for the smaller
element

    for (int j = low; j <= high - 1; j++) {
        if (arr[j] < pivot) {
            i++;
            swap(arr[i], arr[j]);
        }
    }
    swap(arr[i + 1], arr[high]);   // Swap the
pivot element with the element at i+1
    return i + 1;
}


// QuickSort function
void quickSort(vector<int>& arr, int low, int
high) {
    if (low < high) {
        int pi = partition(arr, low, high);   //
Find the pivot index

        quickSort(arr, low, pi - 1);      //
Recursively sort the left subarray
```

```cpp
        quickSort(arr,  pi  +  1,  high);      //
Recursively sort the right subarray
    }
}


int main() {
    vector<int> arr = {38, 27, 43, 3, 9, 82, 10};

    cout << "Original array: ";
    for (int num : arr) {
        cout << num << " ";
    }
    cout << endl;

    quickSort(arr, 0, arr.size() - 1);

    cout << "Sorted array: ";
    for (int num : arr) {
        cout << num << " ";
    }
    cout << endl;

    return 0;
}
```

Explanation:

- The quickSort function chooses a pivot and partitions the array around it.

227

- The `partition` function rearranges the array so that elements smaller than the pivot are on the left and elements greater than the pivot are on the right.
- QuickSort is generally more efficient than Merge Sort in practice due to its smaller overhead, and its average time complexity is **O(n log n)**. However, in the worst case, it can degrade to **O(n^2)** if the pivot selection is poor.

Real-World Application: Sorting Large Datasets

One of the most common real-world applications of **divide and conquer** algorithms, especially **Merge Sort** and **QuickSort**, is in **sorting large datasets**. Sorting is a fundamental operation in computing, and efficient sorting algorithms are crucial for handling large amounts of data.

For example, consider a **big data** scenario where you need to sort millions or billions of records in a database or a file system. Sorting such large datasets efficiently is key to improving query response times, data retrieval speeds, and overall system performance.

- **Merge Sort** is preferred when stability (i.e., preserving the relative order of equal elements) is important or when working with large datasets that don't fit into memory (because Merge Sort works well with external storage).

228

- **QuickSort** is often used when memory usage is a concern, and when data can fit into memory, as it generally performs better in practice.

Both algorithms are frequently used in libraries and systems for tasks like:

- **Database indexing**: Sorting records in a table.
- **File sorting**: Sorting files based on some attributes.
- **MapReduce** systems: Sorting large distributed datasets efficiently.

Conclusion

In this chapter, we explored **divide and conquer** algorithms, focusing on **Merge Sort** and **QuickSort**, which are both efficient algorithms for sorting. We implemented these algorithms in C++ and saw how they can be used to sort data in **O(n log n)** time. Additionally, we discussed the **real-world application** of these algorithms in **sorting large datasets**, highlighting their importance in fields like **big data**, **database management**, and **file systems**. By understanding divide and conquer techniques, you can solve a wide range of problems that involve sorting, searching, and optimization.

CHAPTER 21

BACKTRACKING – FINDING ALL SOLUTIONS

In this chapter, we will explore **backtracking**, an algorithmic technique for solving problems by building up solutions incrementally and abandoning solutions as soon as we determine that they cannot lead to a valid solution. Backtracking is a general approach that is used to find all solutions to combinatorial problems. We will discuss how backtracking works, solve classic problems like the **N-Queens problem** and a **Sudoku solver**, and explore a **real-world example** in **puzzle solving applications**.

Explanation of Backtracking Techniques

Backtracking is a **recursive algorithmic technique** used to solve problems that require exploring all possible solutions. The idea is to build a solution step-by-step and to abandon (or **backtrack**) as soon as it is determined that the current partial solution cannot lead to a valid or optimal solution.

Key Concepts of Backtracking:

1. **Choice**: At each step, the algorithm makes a choice from a set of options.

2. **Constraints**: After each choice, the algorithm checks whether the current solution satisfies the problem's constraints.

3. **Backtrack**: If the current solution doesn't lead to a valid or optimal solution, the algorithm **backtracks**, undoing the most recent choice and trying another option.

4. **Solution**: If a valid solution is found, the algorithm records the solution and may continue to search for other solutions.

Backtracking is often used for problems involving **searching**, **combinations**, **permutations**, and **constraint satisfaction**.

Solving Problems with Backtracking

We will look at two classic problems that are often solved using backtracking: the **N-Queens problem** and the **Sudoku solver**.

---

1. The N-Queens Problem

The **N-Queens problem** is a classic problem where the goal is to place **N queens** on an **N×N chessboard** such that no two queens threaten each other. That is, no two queens can share the same row, column, or diagonal.

Steps to Solve:

1. Start by placing queens one by one in the rows.
2. For each queen, try placing it in all columns of the current row and check if it is safe to place the queen there.
3. If the placement is valid, move to the next row and repeat the process.
4. If placing the queen in a column leads to a conflict later, backtrack and try the next column.

C++ Code for the N-Queens Problem Using Backtracking:

cpp

```cpp
#include <iostream>
#include <vector>
using namespace std;

class NQueens {
private:
    int N;
    vector<vector<int>> board;

    // Function to check if a queen can be placed
at position (row, col)
    bool isSafe(int row, int col) {
```

232

```cpp
    // Check the column
    for (int i = 0; i < row; i++) {
        if (board[i][col] == 1) {
            return false;
        }
    }


    // Check upper-left diagonal
    for (int i = row - 1, j = col - 1; i >=
0 && j >= 0; i--, j--) {
        if (board[i][j] == 1) {
            return false;
        }
    }


    // Check upper-right diagonal
    for (int i = row - 1, j = col + 1; i >=
0 && j < N; i--, j++) {
        if (board[i][j] == 1) {
            return false;
        }
    }


    return true;
}


// Function to solve the N-Queens problem
using backtracking
    bool solve(int row) {
```

233

```cpp
        if (row == N) {
            return true;    // All queens are
placed
        }

        for (int col = 0; col < N; col++) {
            if (isSafe(row, col)) {
                board[row][col] = 1;    // Place
queen
                if (solve(row + 1)) {
                    return true;    // If placing
queen leads to a solution
                }
                board[row][col] = 0;        //
Backtrack
            }
        }

        return false;  // No valid position found
    }

public:
    NQueens(int    N)    :    N(N),    board(N,
vector<int>(N, 0)) {}

    void solveNQueens() {
        if (solve(0)) {
            for (int i = 0; i < N; i++) {
                for (int j = 0; j < N; j++) {
```

234

```
                  cout << (board[i][j] ? "Q "
: ". ");
            }
            cout << endl;
        }
    } else {
        cout << "No solution exists!" <<
endl;
    }
    }
};

int main() {
    int N = 8;  // Example with 8 queens
    NQueens nQueens(N);
    nQueens.solveNQueens();
    return 0;
}
```

Explanation:

- The `isSafe` function checks if it is safe to place a queen at position (`row, col`) by ensuring that no queens are already placed in the same column or diagonal.

- The `solve` function attempts to place queens in each column of a row and recursively moves to the next row. If a valid solution is found, it returns `true`. If no solution can be found in a column, it backtracks and tries the next column.

Output for N = 4:

css

```
. Q . .
. . . Q
Q . . .
. . Q .
```

---

2. Sudoku Solver

The **Sudoku solver** is a common problem that can be efficiently solved using backtracking. The goal is to fill a **9×9 grid** with digits from 1 to 9 such that:

- Each row contains each digit exactly once.
- Each column contains each digit exactly once.
- Each of the nine 3×3 subgrids contains each digit exactly once.

Steps to Solve:

1. Find the first empty cell in the grid.
2. Try placing digits from 1 to 9 in the empty cell, checking if the placement satisfies all the Sudoku rules.
3. If the digit is valid, recursively solve the next empty cell.
4. If no valid digit can be placed, backtrack to the previous step and try a different digit.

236

C++ Code for Sudoku Solver Using Backtracking:

cpp

```cpp
#include <iostream>
#include <vector>
using namespace std;

class SudokuSolver {
private:
    vector<vector<int>> board;

    // Function to check if placing num at (row,
col) is valid
    bool isValid(int row, int col, int num) {
        // Check row
        for (int i = 0; i < 9; i++) {
            if (board[row][i] == num) {
                return false;
            }
        }

        // Check column
        for (int i = 0; i < 9; i++) {
            if (board[i][col] == num) {
                return false;
            }
        }

        // Check 3x3 subgrid
```

237

```cpp
        int startRow = row - row % 3;
        int startCol = col - col % 3;
        for (int i = startRow; i < startRow + 3;
i++) {
            for (int j = startCol; j < startCol
+ 3; j++) {
                if (board[i][j] == num) {
                    return false;
                }
            }
        }

        return true;
    }

    // Function to solve the Sudoku using
backtracking
    bool solveSudoku() {
        int row, col;
        bool emptyCell = false;
        for (row = 0; row < 9; row++) {
            for (col = 0; col < 9; col++) {
                if (board[row][col] == 0) {
                    emptyCell = true;
                    break;
                }
            }
            if (emptyCell) break;
        }
```

```cpp
        if (!emptyCell) {
            return true;   // No empty cells,
puzzle is solved
        }

        // Try placing numbers from 1 to 9
        for (int num = 1; num <= 9; num++) {
            if (isValid(row, col, num)) {
                board[row][col] = num;
                if (solveSudoku()) {
                    return true;
                }
                board[row][col]   =   0;        //
Backtrack
            }
        }

        return false;   // No valid number can be
placed
    }

public:
    SudokuSolver(vector<vector<int>>&  board)   :
board(board) {}

    void solve() {
        if (solveSudoku()) {
            for (int i = 0; i < 9; i++) {
```

```cpp
            for (int j = 0; j < 9; j++) {
                cout << board[i][j] << " ";
            }
            cout << endl;
        }
    } else {
        cout << "No solution exists!" <<
endl;
    }
    }
};


int main() {
    vector<vector<int>> board = {
        {5, 3, 0, 0, 7, 0, 0, 0, 0},
        {6, 0, 0, 1, 9, 5, 0, 0, 0},
        {0, 9, 8, 0, 0, 0, 0, 6, 0},
        {8, 0, 0, 0, 6, 0, 0, 0, 3},
        {4, 0, 0, 8, 0, 3, 0, 0, 1},
        {7, 0, 0, 0, 2, 0, 0, 0, 6},
        {0, 6, 0, 0, 0, 0, 2, 8, 0},
        {0, 0, 0, 4, 1, 9, 0, 0, 5},
        {0, 0, 0, 0, 8, 0, 0, 7, 9}
    };

    SudokuSolver solver(board);
    solver.solve();

    return 0;
```

```
}
```

Explanation:

- The `isValid` function checks if placing a number in a specific cell satisfies the Sudoku rules.
- The `solveSudoku` function recursively places digits in empty cells, backtracking when it finds no valid options.
- The board is displayed once the puzzle is solved.

Real-World Example: Puzzle Solving Applications

Backtracking is often used in **puzzle solving applications**, where the goal is to explore all possible configurations of a puzzle and find a valid solution. For example:

- **Sudoku solvers** (as demonstrated above) use backtracking to fill in the grid while ensuring that the puzzle constraints are satisfied.
- **N-Queens** and other constraint satisfaction problems use backtracking to explore all possible placements of queens on a chessboard, ensuring that no two queens threaten each other.
- **Crossword puzzle solvers** can use backtracking to fill in a grid while ensuring that the words formed horizontally and vertically match the given clues.

241

Conclusion

In this chapter, we explored **backtracking**, a recursive algorithmic technique for finding all solutions to a problem by incrementally building a solution and backtracking when a solution cannot be completed. We solved classic problems like the **N-Queens problem** and **Sudoku solver**, both of which are widely used examples of constraint satisfaction problems. We also discussed **real-world applications** in **puzzle solving**, demonstrating the utility of backtracking in solving complex problems with multiple possible solutions. By understanding backtracking, you can apply this technique to a wide range of problems that require exploring all possible configurations.

CHAPTER 22

BIT MANIPULATION –
EFFICIENT USE OF MEMORY

In this chapter, we will explore **bit manipulation**, a technique used to manipulate individual bits of data in an efficient and space-saving manner. Bit manipulation is often used to solve problems in areas like **memory optimization, algorithmic performance**, and **low-level system programming**. We will discuss the fundamental **bitwise operations**, their applications in solving problems, and a **real-world example** in **data compression algorithms**.

Introduction to Bitwise Operations and Manipulation

Bitwise operations operate directly on the binary representation of integers, where each bit (0 or 1) represents a part of the data. These operations are very efficient and are typically faster than arithmetic operations, making them useful in optimizing performance, especially when dealing with large datasets or systems with limited resources.

The most common **bitwise operators** in C++ are:

1. **AND (&)**: Performs a logical AND on each bit of the operands.
    - o   Example: a & b
    - o   Result: Each bit of the result is 1 if the corresponding bits of both a and b are 1, otherwise 0.

2. **OR (|)**: Performs a logical OR on each bit of the operands.
    - o   Example: a | b
    - o   Result: Each bit of the result is 1 if at least one of the corresponding bits of a or b is 1.

3. **XOR (^)**: Performs a logical XOR on each bit of the operands.
    - o   Example: a ^ b
    - o   Result: Each bit of the result is 1 if the corresponding bits of a and b are different, otherwise 0.

4. **NOT (~)**: Inverts all the bits of the operand.
    - o   Example: ~a
    - o   Result: Inverts each bit of a, turning 0 into 1 and 1 into 0.

5. **Left Shift (<<)**: Shifts the bits of the operand to the left by the specified number of positions.
    - o   Example: a << 2
    - o   Result: Shifts the bits of a to the left by 2 positions, filling the empty positions with 0.

6. **Right Shift (>>)**: Shifts the bits of the operand to the right by the specified number of positions.

  o Example: a >> 2

  o Result: Shifts the bits of a to the right by 2 positions, and the empty positions are filled with 0 (or 1 for signed numbers).

These operations allow us to efficiently manipulate data at the bit level, and are commonly used in situations where memory or processing power is limited.

Applications of Bit Manipulation

Bit manipulation is often used for problems that require **efficient use of memory** or **optimized algorithms**. Below are some common applications of bit manipulation:

1. Checking Even/Odd Numbers

Checking whether a number is **even** or **odd** can be done efficiently using the **bitwise AND** operator. The least significant bit (LSB) of an even number is 0, and for an odd number, the LSB is 1. Therefore, we can use the following bitwise expression:

- **Even check**: n & 1 == 0 (if the least significant bit is 0, the number is even).
- **Odd check**: n & 1 == 1 (if the least significant bit is 1, the number is odd).

C++ Code Example:

cpp

```cpp
#include <iostream>
using namespace std;

bool isEven(int n) {
    return (n & 1) == 0;
}

bool isOdd(int n) {
    return (n & 1) == 1;
}

int main() {
    int num = 5;
    cout << num << " is " << (isEven(num) ? "Even"
: "Odd") << endl;   // Output: Odd
    return 0;
}
```

Explanation:

- The bitwise operation n & 1 checks the least significant bit of the number.

- If it is 0, the number is even; if it is 1, the number is odd.

2. Checking if a Number is a Power of Two

A number is a **power of two** if it has exactly one 1 bit in its binary representation. For example, the binary representation of 4 is 100, and the binary representation of 8 is 1000.

To check if a number is a power of two, we can use the following property:

- A number n is a power of two if and only if (n & (n - 1)) == 0 and n > 0.

C++ Code Example:

cpp

```
#include <iostream>
using namespace std;

bool isPowerOfTwo(int n) {
    return (n > 0) && (n & (n - 1)) == 0;
}

int main() {
```

```
    int num = 16;
    cout << num << " is " << (isPowerOfTwo(num)
? "a power of two" : "not a power of two") <<
endl;  // Output: a power of two
    return 0;
}
```

Explanation:

- The expression (n & (n - 1)) will be 0 if n is a power of two, because n - 1 will flip all the bits after the most significant 1 bit in n.
- For example, for n = 8 (binary 1000), n - 1 = 7 (binary 0111), and 8 & 7 = 0.

---

3. Swapping Two Numbers Without Using a Temporary Variable

Bit manipulation can be used to swap two numbers without using a temporary variable. We use the **XOR** operator to achieve this:

Steps:

1. a = a ^ b – The first step combines the two numbers using XOR.
2. b = a ^ b – This step gives us the original value of a.
3. a = a ^ b – Finally, this step gives us the original value of b.

C++ Code Example:

cpp

```cpp
#include <iostream>
using namespace std;

void swap(int& a, int& b) {
    a = a ^ b;
    b = a ^ b;
    a = a ^ b;
}

int main() {
    int x = 5, y = 10;
    cout << "Before swap: x = " << x << ", y = "
<< y << endl;
    swap(x, y);
    cout << "After swap: x = " << x << ", y = "
<< y << endl;   // Output: x = 10, y = 5
    return 0;
}
```

Explanation:

- XOR operation allows us to swap two variables without needing a temporary variable.

Real-World Example: Data Compression Algorithms

One of the most common real-world applications of **bit manipulation** is in **data compression algorithms**, which aim to reduce the size of data for storage or transmission purposes. Compression algorithms often operate on **bits** directly to store data more efficiently, exploiting redundancy in the data.

Huffman Encoding (discussed earlier in Chapter 19) is an example of a **lossless data compression algorithm** that uses **bitwise operations**. It assigns shorter codes to more frequent characters, thus reducing the overall number of bits required to represent the data.

Other Compression Techniques Using Bit Manipulation:

1. **Run-Length Encoding (RLE)**: This algorithm encodes consecutive identical characters as a single character followed by its count. Bit manipulation is used to efficiently encode and decode the counts.

2. **Arithmetic Coding**: A form of entropy encoding where an entire message is represented by a single number between 0 and 1, and bit manipulation is used to encode this number.

Example:

- In **image compression**, techniques like **JPEG** or **PNG** use **bit manipulation** to represent pixel data more efficiently, reducing the size of image files while retaining image quality.

Conclusion

In this chapter, we explored **bit manipulation**, a technique that allows for efficient use of memory and performance optimization by operating on individual bits. We covered common bitwise operations like **AND**, **OR**, **XOR**, and **shift operations**, and demonstrated how these operations can be used in practical applications like checking if a number is even or odd, determining if a number is a power of two, and swapping two numbers. Additionally, we discussed a **real-world example** of **data compression algorithms**, where bit manipulation plays a critical role in reducing the size of data for storage and transmission. By mastering bit manipulation, you can optimize your algorithms and solve problems in a more memory-efficient manner.

CHAPTER 23

ADVANCED DATA STRUCTURES – TRIE AND SEGMENT TREE

In this chapter, we will delve into two advanced data structures: **Trie** and **Segment Tree**. These data structures are particularly useful for solving specialized problems that require efficient searching, querying, and manipulation of data. We will explain the **Trie** data structure, demonstrate how to implement **Segment Trees** for range queries, and explore a **real-world example** of how these data structures are used in **efficient search in large datasets** such as **autocomplete features**.

Understanding Trie Data Structures

A **Trie** (also called a **prefix tree**) is a specialized tree-like data structure that is used for storing a dynamic set or associative array where the keys are usually **strings**. It is particularly efficient for tasks like **searching for prefixes**, **auto-completion**, and **spell checking**.

Key Characteristics of a Trie:

1. Each node represents a **character** in the string.

252

2. The **root node** is an empty node (it does not represent any character).

3. The **edges** between nodes represent characters, and a path from the root to a node represents a prefix of the string.

4. Each string is stored along a unique path in the trie, which helps to reduce unnecessary comparisons.

5. Tries are commonly used when there is a need to quickly find strings that share common prefixes.

Advantages of Tries:

- **Efficient Prefix Searching**: A trie allows for fast searching of strings based on their prefixes.
- **Memory Efficiency**: For datasets with common prefixes, tries can save space by sharing common prefixes among strings.

Operations:

- **Insert**: Add a word to the Trie.
- **Search**: Check if a word or a prefix exists in the Trie.
- **Delete**: Remove a word from the Trie.
- **Prefix Search**: Find all words that start with a given prefix.

C++ Code for Implementing a Trie

Here's a simple implementation of a **Trie** for **inserting** and **searching** words.

```cpp
#include <iostream>
#include <unordered_map>
using namespace std;

class TrieNode {
public:
    unordered_map<char, TrieNode*> children;
    bool isEndOfWord;

    TrieNode() {
        isEndOfWord = false;
    }
};

class Trie {
private:
    TrieNode* root;

public:
    Trie() {
        root = new TrieNode();
    }
```

```cpp
    // Insert a word into the Trie
    void insert(string word) {
        TrieNode* current = root;
        for (char c : word) {
            if    (current->children.find(c)    ==
current->children.end()) {
                current->children[c]    =    new
TrieNode();
            }
            current = current->children[c];
        }
        current->isEndOfWord = true;  // Mark the
end of the word
    }


    // Search for a word in the Trie
    bool search(string word) {
        TrieNode* current = root;
        for (char c : word) {
            if    (current->children.find(c)    ==
current->children.end()) {
                return false;
            }
            current = current->children[c];
        }
        return current->isEndOfWord;  // Return
true if the word exists
    }
```

```cpp
    // Check if there's any word in the Trie that
starts with the given prefix
    bool startsWith(string prefix) {
        TrieNode* current = root;
        for (char c : prefix) {
            if   (current->children.find(c)   ==
current->children.end()) {
                return false;
            }
            current = current->children[c];
        }
        return  true;   // Return  true  if  the
prefix exists
    }
};

int main() {
    Trie trie;

    trie.insert("apple");
    trie.insert("app");
    trie.insert("banana");

    cout   <<   "Search   for   'apple':   "   <<
(trie.search("apple") ? "Found" : "Not Found") <<
endl;   // Found
```

```
    cout << "Search for 'app': " <<
(trie.search("app") ? "Found" : "Not Found") <<
endl;        // Found
    cout << "Search for 'appl': " <<
(trie.search("appl") ? "Found" : "Not Found") <<
endl;     // Not Found
    cout << "Prefix search for 'ban': " <<
(trie.startsWith("ban") ? "Exists" : "Does not
exist") << endl;   // Exists

    return 0;
}
```

Explanation:

- **Insert**: The `insert` function adds a word to the Trie. It checks if a character is already in the children of the current node; if not, it creates a new node.
- **Search**: The `search` function checks if a word exists in the Trie by following the characters of the word.
- **startsWith**: This function checks if there is any word in the Trie that starts with a given prefix.

Implementing Segment Trees for Range Queries

A **Segment Tree** is a binary tree used for storing intervals or segments. It allows for efficient querying of range-based problems, such as **range sum queries**, **range minimum/maximum queries**, and **range updates**. Segment Trees are particularly useful for problems where you need to repeatedly perform queries and updates on an array or list.

Key Operations:

1. **Build**: Construct the segment tree from the input data.
2. **Query**: Find information about a given range of elements (e.g., sum, minimum, or maximum).
3. **Update**: Modify a specific element in the array, and update the tree accordingly.

Time Complexity:

- Building the segment tree: **O(n)**
- Querying the segment tree: **O(log n)**
- Updating the segment tree: **O(log n)**

C++ Code for Segment Tree (Range Sum Query)

Here's an implementation of a **Segment Tree** to handle **range sum queries** and **point updates**.

cpp

```
#include <iostream>
```

258

```cpp
#include <vector>
using namespace std;

class SegmentTree {
private:
    vector<int> tree;
    int n;

    // Build the segment tree
    void build(vector<int>& arr, int node, int start, int end) {
        if (start == end) {
            tree[node] = arr[start];    // Leaf node stores the value of the array
        } else {
            int mid = (start + end) / 2;
            build(arr, 2 * node + 1, start, mid);
            build(arr, 2 * node + 2, mid + 1, end);
            tree[node] = tree[2 * node + 1] + tree[2 * node + 2];  // Internal node stores sum of its children
        }
    }

    // Query the sum in a range [L, R]
    int query(int node, int start, int end, int L, int R) {
        if (R < start || end < L) {
```

```cpp
        return 0;   // No overlap
    }
    if (L <= start && end <= R) {
        return tree[node];   // Total overlap
    }
    // Partial overlap
    int mid = (start + end) / 2;
    int leftSum = query(2 * node + 1, start,
mid, L, R);
    int rightSum = query(2 * node + 2, mid +
1, end, L, R);
    return leftSum + rightSum;
}


// Update the value at index idx
void update(int node, int start, int end, int
idx, int val) {
    if (start == end) {
        tree[node] = val;   // Leaf node
    } else {
        int mid = (start + end) / 2;
        if (start <= idx && idx <= mid) {
            update(2 * node + 1, start, mid,
idx, val);
        } else {
            update(2 * node + 2, mid + 1,
end, idx, val);
        }
```

```cpp
            tree[node] = tree[2 * node + 1] +
tree[2 * node + 2];  // Update internal node
        }
    }

public:
    SegmentTree(vector<int>& arr) {
        n = arr.size();
        tree.resize(4 * n);
        build(arr, 0, 0, n - 1);
    }

    // Query the sum of range [L, R]
    int rangeQuery(int L, int R) {
        return query(0, 0, n - 1, L, R);
    }

    // Update the value at index idx
    void pointUpdate(int idx, int val) {
        update(0, 0, n - 1, idx, val);
    }
};

int main() {
    vector<int> arr = {1, 3, 5, 7, 9, 11};
    SegmentTree segTree(arr);
```

```
    cout << "Sum of values in range [1, 3]: " <<
segTree.rangeQuery(1, 3) << endl;   // Output: 15
(3+5+7)

    segTree.pointUpdate(1, 10);   // Update index
1 with value 10
    cout << "Sum of values in range [1, 3] after
update: " << segTree.rangeQuery(1, 3) << endl;
// Output: 22 (10+5+7)

    return 0;
}
```

Explanation:

- The `build` function constructs the segment tree by recursively dividing the array into subarrays and storing their sums in the tree.

- The `query` function performs a range sum query by checking for the overlap of the queried range with the current segment. It recursively queries the left and right children of the current node.

- The `update` function updates a single element in the array and updates the relevant nodes in the tree to reflect the change.

Real-World Example: Efficient Search in Large Datasets (Autocomplete Feature)

A **real-world application** of **Trie** and **Segment Trees** can be found in **autocomplete systems**. When a user types a query in a search engine or text editor, the system often needs to provide real-time suggestions based on the user's input. These suggestions are typically based on a large dataset (e.g., a dictionary of words or search history).

1. **Trie**: A Trie is commonly used in autocomplete systems because it allows efficient storage and retrieval of words based on their prefixes. When a user starts typing, the system can quickly find all words that start with the current input prefix and suggest them.

2. **Segment Tree**: For handling large datasets or user histories that require frequent range queries (e.g., finding the most popular search queries within a certain date range), a Segment Tree can be used to efficiently process range queries and updates.

For example:

- **Trie** could be used to provide fast autocomplete suggestions as the user types each letter.

- **Segment Tree** could be used to query the frequency of certain keywords over time, enabling real-time filtering based on user activity.

Conclusion

In this chapter, we explored two advanced data structures: **Trie** and **Segment Tree**. The Trie is an efficient structure for prefix-based search operations, commonly used in autocomplete systems and dictionary-based applications. The Segment Tree is an advanced structure used for handling range queries and point updates efficiently, making it suitable for problems that involve large datasets with frequent queries and updates. We also discussed real-world applications, including how these data structures are used for **efficient search** and **data processing** in systems like **autocomplete features** and **range queries**. Understanding these data structures is essential for solving problems involving large datasets and optimizing search and query operations.

CHAPTER 24

DISJOINT SET UNION (UNION-FIND)

In this chapter, we will explore the **Disjoint Set Union (Union-Find)** data structure, a powerful tool used to efficiently handle **equivalence relations** and **connectivity problems** in graphs. We will explain the core concepts behind **Union-Find**, its operations, and how it is used in solving problems like **graph connectivity**. We will also discuss a **real-world example** of using **Union-Find** to model **social network connectivity**.

Introduction to Union-Find Data Structure

The **Union-Find** data structure, also known as **Disjoint Set Union (DSU)**, is used to track a **partition of a set** into disjoint subsets. Each subset is represented as a **set**, and the goal of Union-Find is to efficiently support two main operations:

1. **Union**: Merge two subsets into a single subset.
2. **Find**: Determine which subset a particular element belongs to.

The Union-Find structure is commonly used in problems involving **dynamic connectivity**, such as determining whether two nodes in a graph are connected or not, and for algorithms like **Kruskal's Minimum Spanning Tree (MST)**.

Key Operations:

1. **Find**: This operation determines which subset a particular element belongs to. It follows the chain of parent pointers from the element to the **representative (or root)** of the set.

2. **Union**: This operation merges two subsets into one. It is typically done by linking the smaller set to the larger set to maintain efficiency (called **union by size** or **union by rank**).

3. **Path Compression**: This technique is used in the Find operation to flatten the structure of the tree, making future Find operations faster. It ensures that all nodes directly point to the root.

Applications in Solving Connectivity Problems in Graphs

Union-Find is commonly used to solve problems involving **connectivity** in graphs, where the goal is to determine whether two nodes (or vertices) are connected or to group nodes into connected components.

1. **Connectivity in Graphs**: Given a graph with nodes and edges, Union-Find can help determine if two nodes are connected by a path. By using the **Find** operation, we can check if two nodes belong to the same connected component.

2. **Kruskal's Algorithm for Minimum Spanning Tree**: Union-Find is used to detect cycles in the graph while implementing Kruskal's algorithm. As we process each edge, we use **Union** to merge sets, and **Find** to check if adding the edge would create a cycle (i.e., if the two nodes are already connected).

3. **Dynamic Connectivity**: In dynamic graph problems, where edges may be added or removed, Union-Find efficiently maintains and updates the connectivity information of the graph.

Time Complexity:

- **Find**: $O(\alpha(n))$ (almost constant time, where $\alpha(n)$ is the inverse Ackermann function, which grows extremely slowly).
- **Union**: $O(\alpha(n))$ (using union by size or rank).
- With **path compression** and **union by rank**, the Union-Find operations become very efficient, even for large graphs.

C++ Code Implementation of Union-Find

Here's how the **Union-Find** data structure can be implemented in C++ using the **path compression** and **union by rank** techniques.

cpp

```cpp
#include <iostream>
#include <vector>
using namespace std;

class UnionFind {
private:
    vector<int> parent, rank;

public:
    // Constructor to initialize the Union-Find
data structure
    UnionFind(int size) {
        parent.resize(size);
        rank.resize(size, 0);
        for (int i = 0; i < size; i++) {
            parent[i] = i;   // Initially, each
element is its own parent
        }
    }

    // Find with path compression
    int find(int x) {
```

```cpp
    if (parent[x] != x) {
        parent[x] = find(parent[x]);  // Path
compression: flatten the tree
    }
    return parent[x];
}


// Union by rank (size)
void unionSets(int x, int y) {
    int rootX = find(x);
    int rootY = find(y);

    if (rootX != rootY) {
        // Union by rank: attach the smaller
tree under the larger tree
        if (rank[rootX] > rank[rootY]) {
            parent[rootY] = rootX;
        } else if (rank[rootX] < rank[rootY])
{
            parent[rootX] = rootY;
        } else {
            parent[rootY] = rootX;
            rank[rootX]++;  // Increase the
rank if both trees have the same rank
        }
    }
}


// Check if two elements are connected
```

269

```cpp
    bool connected(int x, int y) {
        return find(x) == find(y);
    }
};

int main() {
    UnionFind uf(10);   // Initialize Union-Find
for 10 elements

    uf.unionSets(1, 2);
    uf.unionSets(2, 3);
    uf.unionSets(4, 5);
    uf.unionSets(6, 7);

    cout << "1 and 3 are connected: " <<
(uf.connected(1, 3) ? "Yes" : "No") << endl;   //
Yes
    cout << "1 and 4 are connected: " <<
(uf.connected(1, 4) ? "Yes" : "No") << endl;   //
No

    uf.unionSets(3, 4);   // Now 3 and 4 should be
connected
    cout << "1 and 4 are connected: " <<
(uf.connected(1, 4) ? "Yes" : "No") << endl;   //
Yes

    return 0;
}
```

Explanation:

- The `find` function uses **path compression** to ensure that each node points directly to the root of the set.

- The `unionSets` function uses **union by rank** to minimize the height of the tree, ensuring efficient operations.

- The `connected` function checks if two nodes belong to the same connected component.

Real-World Example: Social Network Connectivity

One of the most practical applications of **Union-Find** is in modeling **social network connectivity**. In a social network, users are represented as **nodes**, and **friendships** or **connections** between users are represented as **edges**. The Union-Find data structure can help us efficiently track which users are connected (either directly or indirectly) and manage the merging of user groups when new friendships are formed.

Scenario:

- **User A** and **User B** are friends, so we add an edge between them.

- **User C** and **User D** are friends, so we add an edge between them.

271

- Now, if we want to check if **User A** and **User D** are friends (either directly or through mutual friends), we can use **Union-Find** to efficiently check if they are in the same connected component.

Union-Find is ideal for this situation because we can **union** two users when they become friends, and we can use the **find** operation to check if two users are in the same connected group.

Example: In a social network, we could use Union-Find to efficiently:

- **Find** if two users are connected (i.e., friends or indirectly connected through mutual friends).
- **Union** two groups when users become friends.
- Keep track of the **connected components**, representing distinct groups of connected users.

Conclusion

In this chapter, we explored the **Union-Find (Disjoint Set Union)** data structure, which is used to efficiently handle problems related to **connectivity** in sets or graphs. We discussed the **find** and **union** operations, the **path compression** and **union by rank** techniques, and demonstrated their use with **C++ code**. We also explored **real-world applications**, such as **social network connectivity**, where Union-Find is used to track and manage connections

272

between users efficiently. Understanding Union-Find allows you to solve a wide range of problems involving dynamic connectivity in an efficient and scalable manner.

www.ingramcontent.com/pod-product-compliance
Lightning Source LLC
LaVergne TN
LVHW022338060326
832902LV00022B/4102